OXFORD*Playscript*

:as

Steve Barlow & Steve Skidmore

Tigers on the Prowl

Oxford University Press   1993

Oxford University Press, Walton Street, Oxford OX2 6DP

Oxford   New York   Toronto
Delhi   Bombay   Calcutta   Madras   Karachi
Kuala Lumpur   Singapore   Hong Kong   Tokyo
Nairobi   Dar es Salaam   Cape Town
Melbourne   Auckland   Madrid

and associate companies in
Berlin   Ibadan

Oxford is a trade mark of Oxford University Press

Tigers on the Prowl play and activities
© Steve Barlow and Steve Skidmore 1993

First published by Oxford University Press 1993

A CIP catalogue record for this book is available from the British Library.

ISBN 0 19 831277 6

Typeset by Pentacor PLC, High Wycombe, Bucks.

Printed and bound in Great Britain by
Butler & Tanner Ltd, Frome and London

Contents

Tigers on the Prowl

The Story So Far . . .

This is the second book of plays about the Paper Tigers. If you haven't read the first, **Paper Tigers**, what are you waiting for? Get your teacher to get a copy immediately! Just to give you an idea of what you've been missing . . .

The Paper Tigers – a gang of kids who deliver newspapers for Mr Ali – are Caf (Catherine – the leader of the gang), DG (Derek), Shammy (Shamir), Tealeaf (Pauline), Bazzer (Barry), Sharon (sometimes known as Guts), Kawasaki Joe, Yakki (Gareth), and Rodge-ah (Roger).

In *Paper Tigers*, Yakki asks Mr Ali for a job. He begins to regret this when the others tease him. Mr Ali explains that when he first took over the paper shop he was disliked and mistrusted, too. In fact, when the Tigers found some packets of white powder in the shop store, they just naturally assumed that Mr Ali was a drugs dealer . . .

In *Caf's Baf*, DG encourages Caf to replace her mother's broken bath by nicking the one Mr Ali has just put in his new house. She believes DG's claim that Mr Ali has bought his house to make money by renting it to homeless families. She has a change of heart when Mr Ali explains that the house is for his mother. The police accuse Caf of stealing the bath, but Mr Ali protects her, and Caf finally realizes that she has misjudged him.

A Burn Round the Crem sees the first appearance of Big Mal and his gang: two girls, Spanner and Psycho, and a boy, Meltin' Ice Cream. They deliver papers for Eggie Harris, whose shop is on the Hill Estate. Both they and the Tigers lay claim to a new road, Coleman Crescent, and decide on a contest of champions to settle the issue. Kawasaki Joe challenges Meltin' Ice Cream ('cos nothing moves faster than melting ice cream) to a motorcycle race round the crematorium. When Joe's Vespa blows up, he 'borrows' his brother's hot-shot Kwaker AR50 motorbike, which unfortunately ends up in the canal. If you want to know if Joe wins the race and who gets the Crescent, you'll just have to read the first book!

Now read and act on . . .

Introduction

The Do-It-Yourself Section

In each play you will find a DIY Section. We have put this in so that you have the chance to put forward *your* ideas. You will be asked to make up some scenes about the characters and the situations they find themselves in. To get you thinking, we have suggested some scenes you could explore, but we hope that you will think of your own. (They'll probably be better than ours, anyway!)

When you are reading the plays and get to the DIY Section, you have a choice. You can either skip this and go on to the next scene or begin to work on your ideas.

If you decide to skip the section, don't worry about missing out on the storyline; we have written the plays so that you will not lose the thread of the plot.

If you decide to work on the DIY Section, you can choose to present your ideas in several ways.

Improvisation

You can read about how to set up an improvisation in the Activities section on page 145. In small groups, you can work out your ideas and when you are happy with them, write down what happens and what the characters say. This is called **scripting**. You can then practise your scenes and, when you are happy with them, share them with the other members of your group.

Film & Video

If you have the equipment available, you could film your improvisations on movie film or videotape. This can be exciting as you might be able to do location work by actually filming your work out of school or college. You might even wish to film some of the scenes we have written, with members of the group taking the parts of the characters in the plays.

Radio Play

If you don't have access to film or video equipment, you could produce a radio play instead, using a cassette recorder. Remember that anybody who listens to the play cannot see what is going on, so you will have to help your audience to understand what is happening by using sound effects and detailed descriptions.

Photostory

By using a camera, you can produce a photostory, like the ones you read in comics and magazines. Improvise some scenes and then decide which moments in the scenes you wish to photograph. Plan out your pictures first by producing a **storyboard.** This tells the story in a series of still images, like a still cartoon. (Don't worry about how good your drawing is, stick figures will do fine.) You must do this first, so that you know that the audience will understand the plot. Once you have planned this out, you can take a camera and photograph the scenes.

If you use prints, you could present your story by putting it up on the wall, and writing the words that the characters say underneath the pictures.

If you use slides, you could put on a slide show and record the characters' words on a cassette tape and play this as you show the slides. You can make this type of presentation even more interesting by recording background music on the tape.

These are just a few of the different ways you can use the DIY Section. Think of other ways of presenting your ideas. Be as inventive as possible and don't be afraid to experiment! Most of all, we want you to *enjoy* working on the plays.

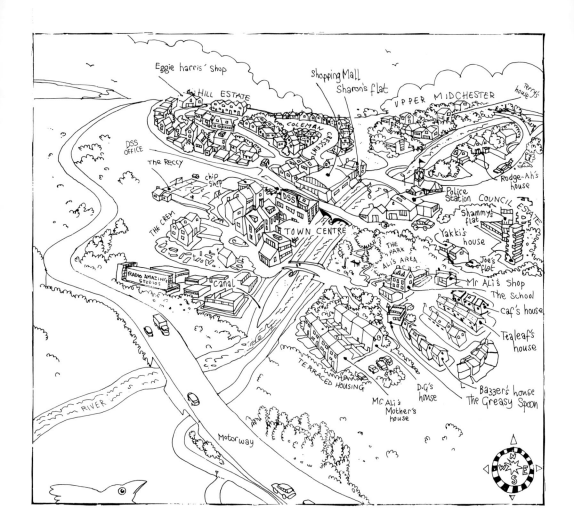

Terry's Tramp

The Characters

Caf
DG
Shammy
Sharon
Kawasaki Joe   *The 'Paper Tigers'*
Rodge-ah
Bazzer
Tealeaf
Yakki-da
'10p' Terry

Mr Ali   *The Tigers' employer:*
owner of the paper shop

The Tramp

Reginald Wibble
Mrs Prendergast   *of the Department of Social Security*

Mike Input   *reporter for Radio Amazing*

Scene 1

Outside the shop. **Yakki** *enters. He stops and looks around.* **Bazzer** *joins him. He is out of breath.*

Bazzer Crikey, I'm cream crackered! Flippin' 'eck, Yakki, I know you've got mountains in Wales, but you went up that hill like it wasn't there. You should be on 'The Krypton Factor'.

Yakki (*Puzzled*) What hill?

Bazzer The hill we just . . . (*He spots* **Terry** *coming in and taking up a position just outside the shop*) Oh no! She's back!

Yakki Who is?

Bazzer I don't believe it. Come on. (*He pulls Yakki's coat*) Get back here quickly. She'll see you else.

Yakki Who will?

Bazzer I thought we'd seen the last of her. But she's back. Like 'Jaws Two'. 'Just when you thought it was safe to go back in the water.'

Yakki Who is she?

Bazzer Who is she? Who is she? You don't know who she is?

Yakki If I did, I wouldn't be asking, would I?

Bazzer Where have you been all your life?

Yakki Criccieth.

Bazzer Bless you. Oh, I see, yeah, I forgot, you're new here. Well, that thing over there is worse than 'Nightmare on Elm Street'. That is '10p' Terry.

Yakki Terry? Her whose job I got?

Bazzer Yup.

Yakki Why do you call her '10p'?

Bazzer	How much you got on you?
Yakki	Dunno. (*He looks*) Thirty pence.
Bazzer	Kiss it goodbye. Watch.

> **Terry** *is lying in wait.* **Shammy** *comes around the corner. He is trapped.* **Terry** *makes a leap and corners him, rattling a collection box.*

Shammy	Terry! You're back!
Terry	(*Suspicious*) What about it? (*She tries to look over her shoulder*)
Shammy	What about what?
Terry	My back.
Shammy	I don't mean 'your back', I mean, 'you're back'.
Terry	You trying to be clever?
Shammy	No, no, honest!
Terry	Okay then, 10p – in here. (*She rattles the box*)
Shammy	Aw, come on, Terry, I'm skint.

> **Terry** *rattles the box.*

Shammy	I come from a poor family, you know that.

> **Terry** *rattles the box.*

Shammy	Terry . . . what is it this time? Not donkey homes. I mean, what use are donkeys?

> **Tealeaf** *appears. She tries to sneak past without being spotted.*

Terry	About as much use as that lump on your face.
Shammy	What lump?

Terry	(*Making a fist*) Coming up!
Shammy	Do you take American Express?
Terry	(*Rattling the box*) Gimme!

> **Shammy** *sighs and puts ten pence in the box.* **Terry** *swings round and rattles the box under Tealeaf's nose before she can escape into the shop.*

Terry	10p, Tealeaf.
Tealeaf	Oh yeah, I'll give it you on the way out.
Terry	Now.

> **Terry** *rattles the box.*

Tealeaf	Tell you what, I'll nick a box of chocolates and you can raffle it.

> **Terry** *rattles the box.*

Tealeaf	Oh, all right. (*She puts ten pence into the box*)
Bazzer	(*To Yakki*) See what I mean?
Yakki	I see what you mean.
Bazzer	Listen, we'll sneak off, wait till she's got her papers, then come back. Tell Ali we're sorry for being late . . .
Terry	(*Shouts*) Come on, Bazzer! You're not invisible, you know! I spotted your beady little eyes ten minutes ago!
Bazzer	Oh no! She's seen us. Bang go my chips.

> **Bazzer** *and* **Yakki** *go round the corner.*

Bazzer	Hiya Terry.

> **Caf** *and* **DG** *arrive. When* **Terry** *sees Caf she tries to hide her box but* **Caf** *has already seen it.*

Caf   Terry! I told you before, no collectin' outside the shop. You collect for everything. It's got to stop!

Terry   It's a good cause, Caf.

Caf   It always is. Lifeboats, hospitals, orphans, flamin' retired pit ponies. Just pack it in, right?

DG   What is it this time? Save a hedgehog? Or bigger? Save the whales?

Bazzer   I like Whales. I hate Scotland, though!

Caf   Shut up, Bazzer, you're not funny.

Terry   Matter of fact, it's for a dogs' home.

Caf   Dogs? Did you say dogs? (*Thinks for a moment*) I like dogs. (*She puts 10p in the box*) Just this once then.

Terry   (*To DG*) You too.

DG   You must be joking!

Terry   Think so? And who sent me a card when I was ill? My mum wants to thank him personally.

DG   (*Unconvincingly*) Card? What card?

Terry   That card with 'Rest in Peace' on the front, and 'Get worse soon, sicko' inside. My mum opened it. Worth 10p not to tell her you sent it?

DG   I never!

                   Terry rattles her box.

DG   Well, as it's a good cause . . .

                   *DG puts 10p in the box, followed by **Bazzer**. **Kawasaki Joe** arrives, sees what's going on and does a quick about turn – but not quick enough.*

Terry	Oi, you, Barry Sheene, I missed you last time. (*She corners him*) That's two lots you owe. 10p, twice . . . that's twenty pence.
Joe	(*Sulkily*) I'm not givin' you nothin', right?
Terry	(*Very friendly*) Joe, have you ever dreamed about riding a really big bike?
Joe	What, like a Kawasaki 1200?
Terry	Yeah. Imagine what it would be like to be doing a ton on it. Like flying.
Joe	(*Getting carried away*) Yeah, brilliant.
Terry	But then you suddenly realize that your brakes have gone. You can't stop. There's a wall coming up.
Joe	Flippin' 'eck!
Terry	Ever thought what it would be like to smash into a brick wall at a hundred miles an hour?
Joe	No.
Terry	(*Rolling her sleeves up and putting her fist in his nose*) Like to find out?
Joe	15p do?
Terry	Twenty.

Joe puts the money in Terry's box.

Terry	(*To Bazzer*) And who's your friend?
Bazzer	Uh, this is Yakki-da.
Terry	(*Threatening*) Oh, so you're the one that's got my round.
Yakki	(*Retreating*) Well, see, what happened was . . .

Mr Ali comes out of the shop.

Mr Ali	What's going on out here? The newspapers are still sitting on the counter. Oh, Terry, it's you.
Terry	Mr Ali . . .
Mr Ali	That explains it, of course. After all, why should I expect you to be delivering papers when you have serious collecting to do?
Terry	Listen, Mr Ali, about my round . . .
Mr Ali	(*To all the others*) Are you going to deliver newspapers this morning, or not?

The others scurry to get their papers.

Mr Ali	Terry, would you also mind getting your papers, please?
Terry	If you think I'm going to let that Welsh wimp . . . hang on, did you say get my papers? You want me to deliver papers?
Mr Ali	That's what I pay you for.
Terry	I thought you'd given my round to him.
Mr Ali	I said he could do it while you were away.
Terry	That's okay then.
Caf	No it isn't! What about Yakki?
Mr Ali	Please let me finish. He can have part of Terry's round and part of Pauline's. With Coleman Crescent, they are too long.
Terry	Which bit of my round is he getting?
Mr Ali	The roads near the by-pass.
Terry	What, them with the long drives? And that really vicious Alsatian on Parkinson Way?
Mr Ali	Yes.

Terry	Well . . . I suppose that's okay. Would you like to donate 10p to the cause, Mr Ali?
Mr Ali	And what is this week's cause, Terry?
Terry	Save the Trees.
Caf	You said it was dogs.
Terry	Well, it is . . . dogs'd be dead unhappy if there weren't any trees, wouldn't they? See, Mr Ali, we want to stop people chopping down trees and turning them into cardboard boxes and tissues . . .
Mr Ali	And newspapers?
Terry	Yeah, well . . .
Mr Ali	Let me see if I understand you correctly. You want me to contribute to a collection, which you're making while you're supposed to be delivering my papers, the object of which is to put me out of business?
Terry	I s'pose that's one way of looking at it . . .
Mr Ali	Maybe next week, Terry. Come on all of you, people want to read their papers with their breakfast, not their lunch.

*The **Tigers** start to leave in groups of two and three. **Mr Ali** goes back into the shop, shaking his head.*

Terry	(*To Yakki*) Let me get my papers, then I'll walk you.
Yakki	Oh, ta very much.
Terry	I can tell you where all the nazzy dogs are. Besides, you haven't given me your 10p yet!

They go.

. . . .

Scene 2

*The park. A park bench. There is a pile of newspapers on it. The **Tramp** is underneath them, but as the scene begins he is completely hidden. **Yakki** and **Terry** come in.*

Yakki	So why do you do all this collecting?
Terry	Someone's got to. I just think of all the people who need help, they depend on me.
Yakki	Don't you enjoy it, then?
Terry	(*Defensively*) Yeah, I suppose so, but that's not *why* I do it.
Yakki	Would you really have belted them?
Terry	Who?
Yakki	Them two, Shammy and Kawasaki Joe?

Terry	No!
Yakki	Then why . . .?
Terry	Look, that lot don't like putting money in my box straight off – they think it'd look soppy if they just coughed up when I asked them – but they know they're going to give me the money in the end, so I never have to hit them, get it?
Yakki	(*Very confused*) Not really . . .
Terry	Forget it then . . . Look, I go this way. If you go down there, you come out on Wogan Avenue. Just watch out for that Alsatian on Parkinson Way. Oh, and there's a poodle on Aspel Drive. It'll have your ankles . . .

> *The newspapers on the bench suddenly lift up. The **Tramp** sits up, coughing his head off. **Yakki** and **Terry** are frightened out of their wits.*

Terry	Wossat?
Yakki	It's a ghost!

> *The **Tramp** rubs his eyes and scratches himself. He is grunting and coughing.*

Yakki	Oh, it's okay, look, it's only an old tramp.
Terry	I nearly had a heart attack! What's he mean, scaring us like that? Oi, you, what did you do that for?
Tramp	Eh?
Terry	I could have had a heart attack!
Tramp	(*Pointing at Terry's bag*) Them papers?
Terry	What?
Tramp	Them papers?

Terry	Oh, yes. So what?
Tramp	Gi'us one.
Terry	Eh?
Tramp	Gi'us a paper.
Yakki	You've got some papers, mister. The first time we saw you, we thought you *was* papers!
Tramp	Damp. Wet. Dew. Cold.
Terry	(*To Yakki*) What's he on about?
Yakki	The papers he's got are wet from the dew, so he's cold. He wants you to give him a dry paper.
Tramp	'S right.
Terry	Damp? From the dew? Does this mean he's been on the bench *all night*?

Yakki shrugs.

Terry	Here, have you been sleeping on this bench all night?

*The **Tramp** nods.*

Terry	That's a disgrace! It's disgusting!
Tramp	Gi'us a paper.
Terry	(*Carried away and completely ignoring the tramp*) It's a scandal! How could anyone let this poor old man sleep out in the open? Where does he live? (*To the Tramp*) Where do you live?
Tramp	(*Shrugs*) Here.
Terry	See, he hasn't even got a home. It's a disgrace!
Tramp	Paper?

Terry	Don't you worry, I'm going to do something about this. I'll get up a petition. Write to my MP. I'll . . .
Yakki	Why not just give him a paper?
Tramp	(*Agreeing*) Yur!
Terry	I can't do that! They're all paid for! They've all got numbers on, look!
Yakki	Tell Ali you dropped one in a puddle, he'll give you another one, take it round at dinner time.
Terry	What about my dinner?
Yakki	All right then, give him 20p out of your box and he can buy himself a paper.
Terry	That's for the trees! Anyway, what about tomorrow? I can't give him a paper every morning, can I?
Yakki	Why not?
Terry	Listen, thicko, what we need to do is to get him properly looked after. (*To the Tramp*) Don't worry, I'll sort it out. I'm going to fix it . . .

Terry marches off.

Yakki	Uh oh, this means trouble. (*He gives the Tramp a paper*) Here you are.
Tramp	Ta. Goo' lad.

Yakki smiles and walks off. The Tramp settles down under his new paper.

· ·

Scene 3

Outside the DSS office. **Terry** *leads the rest of the* **Tigers**, *except for Rodge-ah and Sharon. They are carrying a banner and placards. Except for* **Terry**, *they are not very enthusiastic about this and the placards are trailing on the ground. They are grumbling to themselves.*

Terry   Right, we're here. The DSS.

Joe   What's that stand for?

DG   Dennis Sucks Soup.

There are giggles from the Tigers.

DG   Or, Daphne's Sweaty Socks.

More giggles. **Terry** *grabs DG's shirt front.*

Terry   What, clever clogs?

DG   Er, Department of Social Security.

Terry   Right! And they're supposed to look after people. So why is that old tramp sleeping in the park? That's not looking after people, is it?

The others mumble.

Terry   Is it?

Shammy   Suppose not.

Tealeaf   If you say so.

Terry   Right then.

Caf   I don't know how you talked me into this. Come on, Terry, let's pack it in, we look real dipheads!

Terry   No!

Tealeaf   We're gonna get done if anyone finds out we're skiving school. I'll be grounded until Christmas!

Terry	Stop moaning. Look, I told you all, I came here yesterday . . .
Tealeaf	We know, so does old Doris Morris. You should've heard her at registration yesterday. (*She puts on a teacher's voice*) 'May I take it that poor Theresa has suffered an unfortunate relapse?'
Terry	I'm not bothered about Doris. Here we are, fighting for justice, demonstrating for the cause . . . (*Proudly*) We might even be arrested at any minute!
Tealeaf	What for?
Bazzer	Ooer!
Terry	We're risking our liberty to safeguard our democratic rights!
Yakki	(*To DG*) Where's she get all those long words from?
DG	She's swallowed a dictionary!
Terry	Stop muttering and get on with it. Are we all here? (*She counts them*) Where's Rodge-ah?
DG	He's not coming. He says everyone can have a home if they want one these days and if anyone's sleeping on a bench it's their own fault.
Caf	I'll brain him! If he thinks he can miss this while I'm making a wally of myself . . .
Terry	You can have what's left of him when I've finished with him.

Sharon comes in, panting.

Sharon	Sorry I'm late. I had to do some shopping for my dad.
Terry	I don't believe it. We could have already been arrested and you'd have missed it because you had to do some shopping!
DG	But we haven't been.
Terry	That's not the point . . .
Joe	I still don't see why we have to come here.

Terry   Listen, I came round here yesterday – they threw me out! They treated me like a little kid! Told me they couldn't go round helping every old crumbly and wrinkly . . .

Joe   I bet they didn't say 'crumbly and wrinkly'.

Terry   Look . . .

Joe   It's not respectful.

Terry   Will you belt up! They said he hadn't signed on. How's he supposed to sign on? I bet he can't even write his own name!

Bazzer   Have you asked him?

Terry   No, but the point is, they wouldn't listen to me, right. I told them they were all fascist pigs, and they threw me out!

DG   I wonder why?

Terry   But they can't throw all of us out, can they?

Tealeaf   But what if they call the police?

Terry   Then we can have a sit down demonstration!

Tealeaf   What's that?

Terry   We all sit down on the ground and link arms. Like this. Come on!

> *Terry grabs the two nearest Tigers and forces them on to the floor. The others join her. Bazzer remains standing.*

Terry   See? If they want us out of the way, they have to carry us!

Bazzer   I'm not doing that.

Terry   Why not?

Bazzer   You can get piles sitting on cold pavements. I saw a telly programme about it.

> *The Tigers look startled and hastily scramble up.*

| **Terry** | They probably won't call the police anyway! But if we make enough of a row, they'll have to do something. Let's see that banner. |

Bazzer and Yakki lift the banner. It is made of an old bed sheet. It says, very blotchily, 'DSS Unfair to Tramps'.

Terry	Not bad. Come on you lot, let's see the placards.
Tealeaf	The what?
Terry	The sticks with the signs on, banana brain!

All the Tigers lift placards made of cardboard tacked to broom handles. Joe's broom handle still has a brush on it.

Terry	Joe, why has your handle got a brush head on it?
Joe	Me mum says she wants it back.
Terry	This is supposed to be a serious demo, not a circus. Come on, get them higher. That's it. Right, we're going to march round in a circle.

The Tigers shuffle round, unhappily.

| **Terry** | That's it, come on! Let's wake them up! Sing!
(*Sings*) We shall not, we shall not be moved!
We shall not, we shall not be moved! |

Just like a tree that's growing by the waterside,
We shall not be moved!
We shall not . . .

She stops. No one else has joined in. They are all staring at her.

Terry   What's up with you? Never heard the song?

Caf   Think my dad used to sing it.

DG   Your grandad used to sing it.

Shammy   Our music teacher sings it. She's ninety!

Terry   My mum taught it me. (*Dangerously*) There's nothing wrong with it, is there?

Sharon   (*Doubtfully*) No, no.

Joe   (*At a loss*) How's it go again?

Terry   (*Speaking very slowly and clearly, as if to a small child*)
We shall not, we shall not be moved!
We shall not, we shall not be moved!
Just like a tree that's growing by the waterside,
We-shall-not-be-moved!

Joe   (*After a pause*) That it?

Terry   That's it.

Joe   (*Thinks; mouths the words; then*) Bit boring, innit?

Terry   (*Through gritted teeth*) Just sing it, right? Come on!
(*Sings*) We shall not, we shall not be moved! . . .

The others gradually join in, reluctantly at first, but soon start to enjoy it. By the third chorus they are belting it out and jumping around. They are interrupted by the appearance of a harassed looking man who comes from the DSS office. His name: **Mr Wibble**.

Wibble	What is all this! Stop that noise at once! What on earth is going on? (*He spots Terry*) You! I told you yesterday, we can't do anything for you. Our hands are tied. This is disgraceful!
Terry	So's letting an old man sleep out in the cold.

The others all agree. They are enjoying the situation.

Wibble	There are rules and regulations. Forms to be filled in. The man isn't even registered for work. We don't know his Social Security number, his National Health code, he's not on the housing list . . . according to our records, he doesn't even exist!
Terry	So you're going to let him freeze to death, or starve to death, or both?
Wibble	Well, not as such . . .
Terry	What's your name?
Wibble	(*Confused*) Er, Wibble, Reginald Wibble.
Caf	(*Laughing*) What?

The others roar with laughter.

Terry	Wibble? Come on you lot. (*Sings*) Wibble is a wimp, Wibble is a wimp, Ee-i-addio, Wibble is a wimp!

*The rest join in, except **Joe** who is still trying to get the words of 'We shall not be moved' right.*

Wibble	Be quiet! How dare you! Silence. Shut up!

*The **Tigers** stop singing but remain defiant.*

Wibble	I'm warning you! If you don't listen to reason, I shall fetch Mrs Prendergast!

*The **Tigers** jeer. **Wibble** goes back inside. Led by **Terry**, the **Tigers** sing:*

Tigers	We've got them on the run, we've got them on the run! Ee-i-addio, we've got them on the run!

*Mike Input, a reporter from the local radio, enters. He carries a cassette recorder with a microphone on a lead.**

Mike Input	(*Over the racket*) Excuse me, can anyone tell me who's in charge here?

The noise dies away.

Caf	I am!
Terry	I am!
Caf	Oh, go on then. (*Points to Terry*) She is.
Mike Input	Can you tell me what this is all about?
Terry	I certainly can! That miserable lot in there . . .
Mike Input	Just a minute. (*Turns on recorder*) One-two-three-testing-testing. This is Mike Input reporting for Radio Amazing. I'm standing here outside the DSS offices, where there seems to be a sort of demonstration going on. A group of children . . .
Terry	Teenagers!
Mike Input	Er . . . teenagers are protesting with placards. I'll just have a word with their leader. (*To Terry*) Can you tell me your name please?
Terry	(*Importantly*) Theresa Gertrude Shaw.
DG	(*Sniggers*) Gertrude?

Terry belts him.

Terry	(*To DG*) I'll kill you!
Mike Input	Er, yes, well, could you tell me, Theresa . . .

*If you have a video camera, Mike Input could be a TV reporter with a camera operator.

Terry	Terry.
Mike Input	. . . Er, Terry, can you explain what this is all about?

> *Mr Wibble returns with **Mrs Prendergast**. She looks official and efficient. **Terry** grabs the microphone, strangling Mike Input who has the cord round his neck.*

Terry	I'll tell you what it's about. Victimization! There's this poor old tramp in the park (*The others agree and carry on encouraging her throughout the speech*), and he's got no food and nowhere to go, and he sleeps under newspapers in the rain, and this lot say they can't do anything 'cos he's not on any of their lists, and what we say is, if they don't do nothing, he'll wake up one morning dead.
DG	How can he wake up if he's dead?
Terry	Shut up! And he'll wake up dead and whose fault will that be?

> *The others cheer. **Mike Input** finally manages to snatch the microphone back.*

Mike Input	(*Turning to Mrs Prendergast*) Well, perhaps we could have a word from a spokesman . . .
Mrs Prendergast	Spokes*person*.
Mike Input	. . . Er, spokesperson from the DSS.
Mrs Prendergast	(*Coolly*) There is really no need for all this upset. We would like to thank this young lady for bringing the case to our attention, and I can assure your listeners that it will be fully investigated.

> *The **Tigers** cheer.*

Wibble	But, Mrs Prendergast, you said . . .
Terry	You mean, you'll send someone to the park to see him? Now?
Mrs Prendergast	Certainly.

*The **Tigers** celebrate. **Mrs Prendergast** grabs the microphone from Mike Input. He is again strangled.*

Mrs Prendergast   Let no one believe that we in the DSS are merely a faceless, heartless bureaucracy. Our motto is 'Compassion and Justice for all!'

*The **Tigers** cheer and applaud. **Mrs Prendergast** smiles, waves and turns back towards the office followed by the protesting **Wibble**. The **Tigers** congratulate Terry and each other. **Mike Input** untangles himself and gasps for breath.*

Wibble   But Mrs Prendergast, you said we couldn't spend all the Department's time and energy looking after disgusting old tramps.

Mrs Prendergast   One does not say such things to the Media, Wibble.

Wibble   But you've made me look a perfect idiot!

Mrs Prendergast   Don't be silly, Wibble. No one's perfect! It is no thanks to you that the Department has escaped serious embarrassment. *You* will investigate this case.

Wibble   Me?! I won't do it! Nothing will make me do it!

Mrs Prendergast   (*Sternly*) Wibble!

Wibble   Oh, very well!

***Mrs Prendergast** goes. The **Tigers** collect the protesting **Wibble** and march off. They are pleased with themselves and sing:*

Tigers   'Ere we go, 'ere we go, 'ere we go . . .

*As the song dies away, **Mike Input** speaks into his microphone.*

Mike Input   This is Mike Input, for Radio Amazing, outside the DSS offices, with a broken windpipe.

*Laughing insanely, he removes the cassette
from the machine, pulls the tape out of it and
tries to eat it.*

. . . .

Scene 4

*The **Tramp** is lying on his bench. A **girl** comes
in eating chips. She finishes them except for the
scraps and throws the paper away. She goes.
The **Tramp** watches her go, gets up, grabs the
paper and eats the scraps.
The **Tigers** come in with **Wibble**.*

Terry There he is, come on!

*The **Tramp** sees them and pulls the chips very
close as if he's afraid they'll take them.*

Wibble Look, this is not going to do any good.

Terry He's got rights, right? And you're going to do the right thing and
see him right, 'cos that's only right, right?

Wibble (*Confused*) Right, er, yes. (*He sits on the bench*) Aahh, good
morning, Mr . . . er . . .

Tramp (*Aggressively*) Gerra mi be'!

Wibble I beg your pardon? Look, I'm here to . . .

Tramp (*Louder*) Gerra mi be'!

Wibble What is he saying?

Yakki I think he wants you to get out of his bed.

Wibble His *bed*? Oh, I see. (*He jumps up*) I'm most dreadfully sorry.

Tramp Big nelly.

Wibble Now look here . . . (*To Terry*) Oh, this is impossible.

Terry	(*To Wibble*) Never mind that. (*To Tramp*) This is Mr Wibble. He's from the Social Security.
Tramp	(*Roars*) Whaaaaaaaatt?

*The **Tigers** shrink back.*

Caf	He's throwin' a wobbly!
Tramp	(*Furious*) Sossha scurie? Sossha scurie? Ah don' wan' no sossha scurie. Ah won' tay charry! Am a wokka, yam. Don' wan' no do-gooers. Clairoff! Gan! Gerronartavit!

*Terry and **Wibble** look at each other. Both look at Yakki. **Yakki** explains patiently.*

Yakki	He doesn't want Social Security. He's a worker, and he won't take charity from do-gooders. He wants you to go away.
Terry	The ungrateful, smelly old tramp. Look here, you, do you know what I've been through for you?
Tramp	Who ast ye? Who ast ye t'set sossha scurie on me? Ah nivver ast ye! Interferin' yun baggage!
Yakki	He wants to know who asked you to . . .
Terry	(*Snaps*) I heard! Listen, you silly old fool, don't you know you've got rights?
Tramp	Shtuff me rice. Don' wan no rice. Lee me lone.

*The **Tramp** shuffles off. The **Tigers** except for Yakki look embarrassed and drift off. **Terry** is speechless. **Wibble** stands behind her as she watches the Tramp go.*

Wibble	I tried to tell you. I tried to tell you it wouldn't do any good. You wouldn't listen, though.
Terry	But it shouldn't happen! People shouldn't be living like that!
Wibble	Of course it shouldn't. We'd like to help everyone. But every year we need more money, and every year we face further cuts. Anyway, you can't help someone who doesn't want to be helped.

Terry	But he *needs* help.
Wibble	Perhaps he does, but he doesn't *know* he needs help – not the sort of help we can give, anyway. Some people are scared of us.
Terry	(*Disbelieving*) Scared? Of you?
Wibble	Of the Social Security. Some of them are ashamed of needing help at all. Some are afraid – maybe they've been in a home or a mental hospital, and they're afraid of being sent back. Some of them have problems with drink – or drugs – they're afraid we'll report them to the police. Some of them are afraid of everything, even of people who want to help them. (*Awkwardly*) Well, never mind. It was a good try.

> *He goes.* **Terry** *is crying.* **Yakki** *touches her shoulder.*

Yakki	Come on, Terry. If we hurry we can make afternoon lessons.
Terry	How *dare* he!
Yakki	(*Startled*) What? Wibble?
Terry	That tramp! How dare he? He's not seen the last of me! Right! I know what I'm going to do. I'll set up a collection.
Yakki	Terry, don't you think . . .
Terry	No! I'm going to set up a collection for the miserable old devil, and all you lot are going to help. You're going to do odd jobs and earn lots of money.
Yakki	But . . .
Terry	I'll do him some good, even if it kills me!

> **Terry** *storms off.*

Yakki	Or him . . .

> **Yakki** *follows Terry off, shaking his head in disbelief at her.*

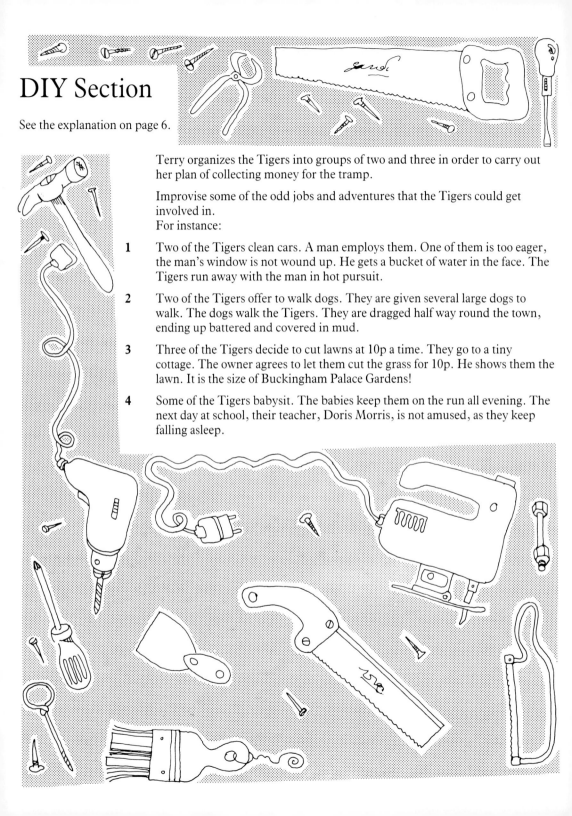

DIY Section

See the explanation on page 6.

Terry organizes the Tigers into groups of two and three in order to carry out her plan of collecting money for the tramp.

Improvise some of the odd jobs and adventures that the Tigers could get involved in.
For instance:

1 Two of the Tigers clean cars. A man employs them. One of them is too eager, the man's window is not wound up. He gets a bucket of water in the face. The Tigers run away with the man in hot pursuit.

2 Two of the Tigers offer to walk dogs. They are given several large dogs to walk. The dogs walk the Tigers. They are dragged half way round the town, ending up battered and covered in mud.

3 Three of the Tigers decide to cut lawns at 10p a time. They go to a tiny cottage. The owner agrees to let them cut the grass for 10p. He shows them the lawn. It is the size of Buckingham Palace Gardens!

4 Some of the Tigers babysit. The babies keep them on the run all evening. The next day at school, their teacher, Doris Morris, is not amused, as they keep falling asleep.

Scene 5

Inside the shop: the paper collecting room.
***Terry** bursts in followed by the rest of the*
***Tigers**, except Rodge-ah.*

Terry   I'll do him! I'm really going to kill him!

*** Caf** comes in behind the others.*

Caf   Who's she on about?

Others   (*Together*) Rodge-ah!

Caf   Right!

Terry   Here's the rest of us, slaving away, knocking ourselves out . . .

Tealeaf   Yeah! I was babysitting for Mrs Trotter last night. That kid! It leaks both ends!

Bazzer   Must be Welsh! (*He laughs. No one else does. He stops, then tries to explain his feeble joke*) Welsh. Leeks both ends. Geddit?

Caf   I've told you before, Bazzer, you're just not funny.

Bazzer   Forget it then.

DG   We have.

Joe   I tried to start a motorbike despatch rider service on me Vespa. Had to pack it in, though. This woman wanted me to take a parcel to her sister . . .

Shammy   Why didn't you?

Joe   . . . In Edinburgh.

Tealeaf   I took some woman's shoppin' home. She must have bought half of Sainsbury's. My arms are twice as long as normal!

DG   This old dear made me weed her path: it was longer than the M1! My back's killing me.

Shammy   Mrs Dickinson said she'd give me 10p if I put a plug on her new toaster, but when I switched it on, it blew up, so she didn't.

Yakki   What, blow up?

Shammy   Didn't give me 10p, berk head! She was going to make me pay for a new one, but I ran off!

Yakki   I did the washing up for my mum. She wouldn't give me the money 'cos I made her twenty-four piece dinner set into a hundred and ninety-four piece set! I've got to pay for it as well!

        Everyone looks at Terry.

Terry   I supervised!

        Everyone groans.

Terry   And I did the babysitting, and took some bottles back to the shop and . . .

Caf   Okay, okay.

        Everyone looks at Sharon.

Sharon   I swept up the hair at Maria's Hair Salon for a morning.

        *The **Tigers** wait for her complaint.*

Sharon   Actually, I quite enjoyed it!

Caf   (*Disgusted*) Uuurrr! Shut up, Guts.

Terry   But who did absolutely nothing at all?

Others   Rodge-ah!

Caf   Come on then, put it all here, let's see how much we got.

        *They all put their money on the counter. **Sharon** counts it, then counts it again. They wait expectantly.*

Sharon   One pound, thirty-seven and a half pence, three pesetas and a tiddlywink.

Terry   How much?

Sharon	One pound . . .
Terry	Is that all?
Joe	Well, it's enough for fish'n'chips, innit?
Terry	It's pathetic! Listen, you lot . . .
Mr Ali	(*Outside the door*) Will you please get a move on! It's eight o'clock already. That room is for collecting papers, not for holding meetings.
Sharon	Sorry!
Yakki	Sorry, Mr Ali!
Caf	Coming!
DG	On our way!

> *They grab the papers and rush out.* **Mr Ali** *comes in and watches them go. He sighs and straightens the remaining papers. After a few moments,* **Rodge-ah** *comes in, cautiously.*

Rodge-ah	Morning, Mr Ali. Can I have my papers please?
Mr Ali	Ah, Roger.
Rodge-ah	Sorry I'm late.
Mr Ali	You were waiting for the rest to go, I suppose?

> **Rodge-ah** *hangs his head.*

Mr Ali	They aren't very pleased with you, you know.
Rodge-ah	(*Defensively*) I've not done anything!
Mr Ali	That's why they aren't very pleased with you!
Rodge-ah	Well, why should I? I've never met this person. I don't know him. He's just a stinking old tramp. My dad says tramps are parasites.

They just scrounge off people who work hard. My dad says we ought to do away with them.

Mr Ali   Indeed. But how? In my experience, things do not go away because you do not like them.

Rodge-ah   It's none of my business.

Mr Ali   (*Like an actor delivering his lines*) 'Mankind was my business.'

Rodge-ah   What?

Mr Ali   I'm sorry. It's a line from a book. Jacob Marley's ghost says it to Scrooge. 'A Christmas Carol' by Charles Dickens. Have you read it?

Rodge-ah   Charles Dickens? My brother's reading him for GCSE. He says it's very difficult. (*He looks at Mr Ali with new respect*)

Mr Ali   It's a favourite book of mine. Scrooge, you see, is a very mean man. On Christmas Eve, four ghosts appear and show him how his meanness has lost him all his friends and made most good people fear or hate him. He learns his lesson and becomes a friend to the poor.

Rodge-ah   Oh.

Mr Ali   At the beginning, two men come to see Scrooge. They ask him for money to give to poor people. He asks them if there are no prisons or workhouses. They say that many people would rather die than go to such places. Scrooge says, 'If they would rather die, they had better do it, and decrease the surplus population.' Perhaps you'd agree with Scrooge, Roger?

Rodge-ah   (*Troubled*) But it's nothing to do with me.

Mr Ali   (*Calmly*) If you say so, Roger.

Terry *rushes in.*

Terry   Mr Ali, you didn't give me the Radio Times for 37. (*She sees Rodge-ah*) You! Think you're clever, don't you, Rodge-ah? You've got loads of money, so you don't care about poor old men who sleep rough. Well, I'm going to show you. You can take that smile off your face, you're coming with me.

*She grabs Rodge-ah and pulls him out of the shop. **Mr Ali** calls out.*

Mr Ali   Hey! What about my papers?

. . . .

Scene 6

*The park. The **Tramp** is sitting on his bench as **Terry** and **Rodge-ah** enter. He sees Terry and gets up to shoo her off.*

Tramp   Yu! Girroff! Setta sossha scurie on me – don' wan' yer. Lee me 'lone.

He starts to shuffle off.

Terry   Wait a minute, I haven't brought anyone with me. This is only Rodge-ah. He's nobody.

Rodge-ah   Thanks.

Terry   Nobody special. I mean he's not from the Social Security or anything like that. Look, I've got something for you.

Tramp   Eh?

Terry   I've brought you something.

Tramp   (*Pleased*) Brin' me summn?

Terry   Yeah! We had a collection, see.

Tramp   (*Scornfully*) Clesshuns!

Terry   Yes, it's not a lot I'm afraid, but . . . (*She gives him the money*)

Tramp   (*Taking it*) Ta.

Terry   Ta? Is that all? Don't you want it? Aren't you grateful?

Tramp   Waffor? S'not yors. S'clesshun. (*He starts to shuffle off*)

Terry   (*Flustered*) You ungrateful . . . You . . . What *do* you want?

Tramp	(*Delivering a challenge*) Tek m'yome. Yor ows. Cuppa tea.
Terry	(*Horrified*) Take you to my house for a cup of tea? I can't do that! Mum would go bananas!

> The **Tramp** *shrugs and shuffles further off.*

Terry	Wait! Where are you going?
Tramp	Gerra borrl.
Terry	A bottle? That money isn't for drink, it's for food!
Tramp	Norrungry. (*He goes*)

> **Terry** *is close to tears again. She sits on the bench.*

Terry	I don't believe it – after all I've done for him. How can he treat me like this?
Rodge-ah	Me, me, me.
Terry	Shut up, stupid.
Rodge-ah	*I'm* stupid? You're good at calling everyone else names, aren't you? The thing is, Terry, it's *you* that's stupid.
Terry	(*Outraged*) What?
Rodge-ah	After all you've done for him? What have you done for him? Nothing! You did it all for yourself, so *you* could feel good, so that everyone could see how kind *you* are! You're the one that's stupid!
Terry	That's not true!
Rodge-ah	Really? Then why didn't you find out what *he* wanted? Not what you think he wanted? You still don't know, do you?
Terry	And I suppose you do, clever clogs?
Rodge-ah	Of course. It's obvious.
Terry	What then?

Rodge-ah	A friend.
Terry	(*Shocked*) A friend?
Rodge-ah	That's all.
Terry	That's *all*?
Rodge-ah	Not demonstrations, not collections, just a friend.
Terry	Be a friend? To *him*?
Rodge-ah	Why not?
Terry	He's old. He smells.
Rodge-ah	You tried to get others to look after him. Why not yourself?
Terry	At least I did more than you!
Rodge-ah	True.

> The **Tramp** comes back. He is furious to see Terry on his 'bed'.

Tramp	I toad yer. Gerroff!

> The **Tramp** moves forward threateningly. **Rodge-ah** turns and stands his ground. The **Tramp** is puzzled: most people are frightened of him. He tries to frighten Rodge-ah by waving his arms and shouting.

Tramp	Aaaaaaarrrrrrrgggggghhhhhh!
Rodge-ah	Don't you ever clean your teeth?
Tramp	Waaaa?
Rodge-ah	Your breath smells like sweaty socks!
Terry	(*Embarrassed*) Roger!

Rodge-ah	Look at the state of you, you dirty old devil. Is that an orange shirt, or have you spilt tomato soup down it?
Tramp	Yur cheeky yun' beggar . . .
Rodge-ah	I'm ashamed of you!
Tramp	Whurr *yur* ashamed?
Rodge-ah	'Cos if you spent the money that Terry gave you on soap instead of drink, you'd be better off.
Tramp	Shoap?!
Rodge-ah	Yes, if you cleaned yourself up, you wouldn't look so bad.
Tramp	Gi'oor.
Rodge-ah	You wouldn't. Better than stinking of booze and sweat.
Tramp	(*Sulkily*) Go' no booze.
Rodge-ah	Why not?
Tramp	Wooden serve me.
Rodge-ah	I'm not surprised. Give me the money. I'll get you something.
Terry	Rodge-ah! How can you? You're under age. They won't serve you.
Rodge-ah	Shut up! Come on, hand it over.

The **Tramp** *does so.* **Rodge-ah** *goes off.*

Terry	That money wasn't for beer. I don't know what he's doing. He's just irresponsible.
Tramp	You shurrup. He's orright.
Terry	Don't tell me to shut up! Why do you like him better than me? He wouldn't have even come to see you if I hadn't made him!

The **Tramp** *shrugs.*

Terry	Oh, I hate you! I hate everybody!
	She storms out. **Rodge-ah** *passes her as she goes.*
Rodge-ah	What's up with her? Here you are. (*He offers the Tramp a packet*)
Tramp	Shandwishes? Didn't ashk for shandwishes.
Rodge-ah	Well, that's what you've got. They'll do you better than beer. (*Tempting the Tramp*) They're cheese.
Tramp	(*Weakening*) . . . An' pickle?
	Rodge-ah *checks the sandwiches and nods.*
Tramp	(*A last protest*) I want beer!
Rodge-ah	(*Firmly*) You've got sandwiches. Come on.
	Grumbling, but not seriously, the **Tramp** *takes the sandwiches.*
Rodge-ah	Oh no! I'm missing registration. Look, do you promise to eat the sandwiches?
	There is a pause as the **Tramp** *looks at the sandwiches and then at Rodge-ah.*
Rodge-ah	Promise?
Tramp	Promish.
	Rodge-ah *turns to go.*
Tramp	'Ere! You comin' tomorrow?
Rodge-ah	I might.
	Rodge-ah *goes. The* **Tramp** *begins to eat the sandwiches.*

. . . .

Scene 7

*Outside the shop. The **Tigers** are meeting to collect their papers. **Caf** and **DG** are already waiting. **Yakki** and **Bazzer** arrive.*

Bazzer	Hiya.
Caf	Watcher.
DG	Hi.
Bazzer	Peaceful, innit?
Caf	What is?
Bazzer	I was just saying to Yakki – been peaceful here for the past week. No havin' to dodge Terry to get to the shop.
Yakki	No more rattling of the box!
Caf	Yeah. Where is she?

*Tealeaf comes in with **Sharon**.*

Caf	Have you seen Terry?
Sharon	No.
Tealeaf	She gets her papers after we've gone.
Sharon	She's in school, but doesn't talk to anyone.
Tealeaf	Except Angela Chadwick.
Caf	What, grotty Chadwick? Everyone hates her!

***Shammy** and **Joe** drift in.*

Caf	Any of you know what's wrong with Terry?
Shammy	No, I've not seen her.
Joe	No.
DG	Who cares, so long as she stays out of the way?

Caf	Shut up, DG.
DG	What's wrong with that?
Bazzer	Hey, watch out, here she comes.
Caf	Who, Terry?
Bazzer	Yeah! Scram!

*They make to hide but **Terry** comes in before they can get away. They wait for the inevitable collection.*

Terry	Hello.
Shammy	Er, hi, Terry.

They wait. Nothing happens.

Shammy	Where's the collecting box?

***Terry** doesn't answer. **Mr Ali** comes out of the shop but no one notices him.*

Shammy	What is it this week? RSPCA? NSPCC? Save the Ant?
Terry	I've given all that up.

*There is an awkward silence. Then the **Tigers** go into the shop to collect their papers, chatting quietly about Terry's strange behaviour. **Terry** goes up to Mr Ali.*

Terry	I won't be doing any more collecting, Mr Ali.
Mr Ali	Oh? Do you think that's necessary, Terry?
Terry	All the time I thought I was being kind and everything, and I was just being selfish.
Mr Ali	Not altogether. You just wanted other people to do the dirty work. It's a good thing to care about justice, Terry, but it's a better thing to care about people . . .

He is interrupted by the arrival of the
Tramp. **Rodge-ah** *follows him, looking*
pleased but a little embarrassed. The **Tigers**
begin to come out of the shop with their bags.
They watch as the **Tramp** *moves to Terry.*

Tramp   Preshent.

Terry   For me?

Tramp   A tank. I made it.

The present is a cotton reel tank. The **Tramp**
shows how it works. The **Tigers** *gather round.*

Terry   Thank you.

Joe   Wicked! Can you show me how to make one?

Bazzer   I could make one better than that. Saw it on 'Blue Peter', it's dead
easy . . .

Caf   Shut up, Bazzer.

Tramp   Gorra go. Shee yer. (*He goes*)

The **Tigers** *look at Rodge-ah.*

Rodge-ah   He made one for me. He's good with his hands. He's going to show
me how to make unbeatable conkers when the season comes!

Sharon   Hey, it's the Telethon next week, isn't it? We could have a tank
race!

Terry   The what?

Sharon   Telethon. On TV.

Bazzer   Yeah, they raise money for charity.

Terry   Next week?

Sharon   (*Warily*) Er, yeah . . . I just thought that . . .

Terry	Well, what are we waiting for? Caf, DG, you organize the tank race. Shammy, you could do a sponsored bike marathon. Bazzer, Yakki . . .

*The **Tigers** start to scatter.*

Terry	You can have a holding-your-breath-under-water-competition. Hey, where are you lot going? Come back!

*Everyone has gone except **Mr Ali**, **Terry**, and **Rodge-ah**.*

Terry	Well, isn't that just great?
Mr Ali	I'm glad to see you're feeling better, Terry. (*He goes*)
Rodge-ah	(*Awkwardly*) Do you know something, Terry? You're all right.
Terry	Know something, Roger? So are you.

They grin and follow Mr Ali into the shop.

. . . .

One of our Pages is Missing

The Characters

· · · · · · · · · · · · · · · · ·

Caf **DG** **Shammy** **Sharon** **Kawasaki Joe** **Rodge-ah** **Bazzer** **Tealeaf** **Yakki-da** **'10p' Terry**	*The 'Paper Tigers'*
Mr Ali	*The Tigers' employer:* *owner of the paper shop*
Mr Cook **Ms Payne** **Mr Wright** **Mr Hall** **Mr Watts**	*customers of Mr Ali's paper shop*
Mike Input	*reporter for Radio Amazing*
Police 1 **Police 2**	*the long suffering local Law*

Scene 1

Inside the back room of the paper shop.
Shammy, DG, Bazzer, Yakki *and*
Kawasaki Joe *are looking at leftover tabloid*
newspapers. **Rodge-ah** *is looking on.*

Joe	Look at this one on page three!
DG	Where?
Joe	Here.

DG grabs the paper and makes cooing noises.

DG	Cor! Flippin' 'eck!
Shammy	Let's have a look.
DG	No, she's all mine!
Shammy	Come on . . .
DG	Get lost!

*Shammy makes a grab for the paper. There is
a tussle and the paper rips.*

DG	Now look at what you've done, you wally!
Shammy	It was you.
Yakki	Stop arguing! There's loads more here.
Bazzer	(*Reading a tabloid*) Crikey! Have you seen this one? Look at page three! (*He turns the pages over*) And four . . . and five . . . and six . . . and seven! Every page!
Rodge-ah	Where's the news, though? My father says that newspapers like that are just comics for tiny-minded idiots.
DG	What's wrong with them?
Rodge-ah	For a start, they don't have any news in.
DG	Of course they do. That's why they're called *news*papers.

Rodge-ah   So what news is there in that one?

DG   Loads. (*He reads a headline*) 'Neighbours' star in love.

Shammy   (*Reading*) 'EastEnders' star in punch up.

Bazzer   (*Reading*) Star of 'Home and Away' gets married.

DG   (*Reading*) Find out the sexy secrets of the 'Coronation Street' stars.

Rodge-ah   Exactly! What news is there?

DG   That is news.

Rodge-ah   No, it isn't.

Bazzer   Yes, it is. People want to know about these things . . .

Rodge-ah   You might, I don't. I want to know what's happening in the real world, not what's happening in a make-believe TV series to characters that don't really exist.

DG   What are you on about?

Rodge-ah   I want to know about things that are affecting my life.

DG   I'll affect your life in a minute, if you don't shut up.

Bazzer   Hey, there's some more old returns outside. There might be some more good pictures in . . . (*He goes out*)

Rodge-ah   That's all that will be in.

DG   I'll get Caf to sort you out.

                    ***Caf, Tealeaf, Sharon** and **Terry** walk in.*

Caf   Who am I gonna sort out?

DG   Oh, hi, Caf. It's Rodge-ah, he's talkin' stupid again.

Caf   (*To Rodge-ah*) Shut it, wimp! (*She looks at the rest of the boys*) What are you lot doin' here anyway?

The boys are embarrassed. They shuffle the papers away, trying to hide them out of the sight of the girls.

Shammy   Oh, er . . . we were just sorting out the returns.

DG   (*Quickly*) Yeah, that's right.

Caf   You don't usually do that. (*To Joe*) What are you up to?

Joe   Nothin'! Honest!

Yakki   Honest, Caf, we're just sorting out the returns.

Terry   (*Seeing a paper open*) Oh yes? Well, why is that paper open on page three? You were looking at Page Three Girls, weren't you?

DG   We weren't, were we?

Yakki   No.

Shammy   'Course not.

DG   It's just a coincidence that it's open on that page.

Yakki   That's right, a coincidence. Honestly, Caf, cross my heart and hope to die.

Bazzer enters, holding open a paper at page three.

Bazzer   I thought there'd be some good ones. Just look at . . .

He stops. The girls look daggers. The boys realize the game is up.

Terry   Perverts!

Caf   (*To Yakki*) 'Cross my heart and hope to die'? I'm gonna help you keep that promise. (*She moves over to Yakki*)

Yakki   (*Bravely*) Anyway, what's wrong with looking at page three?

Caf   Lots.

Yakki   Like what?

Caf   Loads. It's . . . er . . . it's . . . What *is* wrong?

Terry   I'll tell you what's wrong. (*She picks up the paper and opens it at page three. She shows it to Caf*) Look at that. What do you see?

Caf   (*Confused*) It's a woman, wearing a nelly gay.

Terry   A what?

Caf   A nelly gay.

Terry   You mean a négligé?

The boys burst out laughing.

Caf   Shut it!

Terry   Okay, she's wearing a négligé, but what does she look like?

Caf   Hey?

Terry   Does she look hard? Does she look fierce?

Caf   No, 'course not. She looks dead soft.

Terry   (*Pointing at the boys*) Do you think she could belt one of this lot if they started anything?

Caf   No.

Terry   Do you think she could even sort out Rodge-ah?

Caf   Er, maybe. (*She looks at Rodge-ah and then the picture*) No, not even him.

Terry   Well, millions of men open up the paper every morning to look at page three and they think that all women are like that. Little cuddly dollies, just waiting for a man to tell them what to do.

Caf   (*Outraged*) What?

Terry	They look at those pictures and think that women are just objects and that all males are better than females.
Caf	No male's better than me!
Terry	(*Realizing she's got Caf well and truly on her side*) That's right. It's disgusting. Women having their bodies stared at by stupid men. It's degrading . . .
DG	They get paid for it.
Terry	Does that make it right? Just look at the sort of papers that print these pictures. They're for idiots!
Rodge-ah	(*Quietly*) That's what I said.

> ***Terry*** *grabs a paper and reads out the headline.*

Terry	'Vampire Alien Fish Eats Buckingham Palace.' No one with a brain cell can believe a story like that.
Joe	I believe it.
Terry	Case proved. You haven't even got half a brain cell.
Joe	But it's got to be true; it's in a newspaper.
Sharon	I don't believe anything that's written in newspapers.
Terry	Neither do I. Papers like these exploit people, especially women . . .
DG	I think that's rubbish. You're making a load of fuss about something that's just a laugh.
Terry	Just a laugh, is it? Men look at those pictures. (*Imitates*) Cor, phoor, look at that! (*Normal voice*) Then they see some female walking alone in the dark, and then what happens?

> ***Mr Ali*** *enters. He is holding an attack alarm. As he comes in he lets it off. There is a loud piercing noise and all the **Tigers** leap in the air with shock. **Mr Ali** switches it off and chuckles*

to himself as the **Tigers** *return to normal, checking their ears, pulses and chests to make sure that they are still alive.*

Caf   Flippin' 'eck!

Mr Ali   (*Laughing*) Sorry about that. I couldn't resist it. At least I know that the alarm works.

Yakki   (*Thumps his chest*) Keep going, you fool!

Tealeaf   I think I've gone deaf.

Shammy   Pardon?

Tealeaf   I think I've gone deaf.

Shammy   I can't hear you. I think I've gone deaf.

Mr Ali   Sorry, Shamir. It is effective, though.

Sharon   What is it?

Mr Ali   It's a personal anti-attack alarm, Sharon. As the nights are drawing in, I've been getting worried about you doing your rounds in the dark.

Sharon   Yes, it gets really creepy down at the flats on Ryder Road.

Terry   There's been lots of reports in the papers about women being attacked and assaulted.

DG   (*Sarcastically*) 'I don't believe anything written in newspapers.'

Caf   Get lost, DG.

Mr Ali   Anyway, I thought it would be best if I gave you girls an alarm. I'd feel a lot happier if you each had one. Do you want one?

Terry   I think it's a good idea, Mr Ali, but we were just saying that maybe there wouldn't be all these attacks if there weren't female pin-ups in the papers.

Mr Ali   (*Uncomfortably*) Maybe Terry, I wouldn't know.

Bazzer	Why can't the boys have one?
Caf	You'd better get one now, Bazzer, 'cos I'm gonna attack you if you don't stop being stupid!
Bazzer	Boys get attacked too, don't they, Mr Ali?
Mr Ali	He's got a point, Catherine. Fair enough, Barry, I'll get you all one. I'll go and ring up and increase the order. They should be here in a couple of days.

Mr Ali goes.

Shammy	(*Still digging at his ear with his finger*) They're really loud.
Caf	I'm not frightened of being attacked by a boy.
Terry	But it could be a man who's a lot bigger than you . . .
Sharon	Or it could be more than one. It could be a gang.
Caf	Oh yeah, I hadn't thought of that.
Terry	(*To the boys*) I don't see why you lot should get one. Statistically, more women are attacked than men . . .
Sharon	(*Picking up a paper*) Look, here's a story about a teenage girl being assaulted.
Terry	(*Taking the paper from Sharon*) And see where the story is? Right next to a page three pin-up. Disgraceful! No wonder women get attacked.
DG	You're stupid, you are. I don't care what you think, Terry. We're gonna carry on lookin' at page three, so there!

The boys go.

Terry	We'll see about that.
Sharon	(*To Terry*) D'you really think women get attacked because of page three?

Terry	Well, looking at pictures like that, what do you think blokes will think about?
Tealeaf	We ought to do something about it.
Caf	Yeah. What, though?
Terry	If you lot are serious, I've got an idea. Come here.

The girls go into a huddle.

. . . .

Scene 2

*The paper shop. **Mr Ali** is behind the counter. Two customers, **Mr Cook** and **Ms Payne**, enter.*

Mr Ali	Good morning, Mr Cook.
Mr Cook	Morning. (*To Ms Payne*) Do you want to be served first, gorgeous?
Ms Payne	No thank you. Age before beauty, (*Sarcastically*) gorgeous.

She turns away and begins to look at the magazines on the shelf.

Mr Cook	Er, oh . . . all right, then. Actually, I've got a complaint, Mr Ali.
Mr Ali	(*Concerned*) Oh, yes?
Mr Cook	It's my morning paper . . .
Mr Ali	Hasn't it been delivered?
Mr Cook	Oh yes, it's been delivered. It's just that . . . er . . . there's some of it missing . . .
Mr Ali	You mean one of the supplements?
Mr Cook	No. (*He looks at Ms Payne, then back to Mr Ali. He whispers*) One of my pages is missing.
Mr Ali	Pardon?

Mr Cook   (*Quietly*) One of my pages is missing.

Mr Ali   (*Loudly*) One of your pages? Which one?

Mr Cook   Shhhhh! Er . . . page four. It's been cut out.

Mr Ali   Cut out? Do you have the paper with you?

Mr Cook   Yes, here it is.

He gives Mr Ali the paper. **Ms Payne**, *who has overheard the last part of the conversation, comes to the counter.*

Ms Payne   Been cut out, you say?

Mr Cook   (*Embarrassed*) Oh, er, yes.

Ms Payne   Let me see. Page four, you said?

She grabs the paper.

Ms Payne   So it is. (*Exaggerating*) I wonder what was on page four?

Mr Ali picks up a copy from the counter. **Ms Payne** *takes it from him and turns to page four.*

Ms Payne   Oh well, I wouldn't bother too much, all it is is an advert for MIF furniture. They've got a sale on this week. Funny that, they seem to have a sale on every week. (*To Mr Cook*) Were you thinking of buying some furniture?

Mr Cook	No, er, yes, er, maybe . . .

Ms Payne   (*Very pointedly*) Or perhaps you wanted to see what was on page three. (*Turns over the page and thrusts the picture in Mr Cook's face. He becomes very embarrassed*) I thought so! You dirty old man! Well, don't worry, I'll ask all my friends if they can get hold of a copy for you. If I ask enough people and tell them why you want it, I'm sure they'll let you have one.

Mr Cook   (*Realizing the effect this will have*) No, there's no need to bother, honest, I'm not really bothered . . .

Ms Payne   Men, you're all alike! I'll take a copy of 'Bulging Biceps Monthly', Mr Ali. See how you like us staring at you. (*She looks at Mr Cook*) Although I'm certain you'd never be in it, looking like you do . . . Goodbye, *gorgeous*!

She turns and storms out of the shop.

Mr Ali   I'm sorry about that.

Mr Cook   Yes, well, if I could just have a new copy, please.

Mr Ali   Of course. I'm very sorry, I don't know how it could have happened.

*He gives the paper to **Mr Cook** who puts it under his coat and leaves. Another customer, **Mr Wright**, walks in.*

Mr Ali   Good morning, Mr Wright.

Mr Wright   It's not good at all.

Mr Ali   Why not?

Mr Wright   Look at this . . .

***Mr Wright** holds up a tabloid newspaper and flicks through it. It has had pictures cut out of it. **Mr Wright** looks at Mr Ali through the holes in the paper.*

Mr Wright   How on earth has this happened?

Mr Ali	I haven't a clue.
Mr Wright	Well, it's not good enough!
Mr Ali	From which page have the pictures been cut?
Mr Wright	Which do you think?
Mr Ali	Page three?
Mr Wright	And five and seven and the centre pages. It's disgraceful!
Mr Ali	Yes, I'm sorry. Please, take a new paper.
Mr Wright	I should think so! I expect it to be free, considering the time and effort it's taken me to come here.
Mr Ali	Of course . . .

*Mr Wright leaves as **Mr Hall** and **Mr Watts** walk in holding newspapers.*

Mr Ali	Oh no!
Mr Hall	I'm afraid we've got a complaint, Mr Ali.
Mr Ali	Don't tell me, I can guess what it is. Pictures have been cut from your newspapers.
Mr Watts	That's right, how did you know?
Mr Ali	It doesn't matter . . .

Two more male customers come in. They too are brandishing newspapers.

Mr Ali	(*Muttering to himself*) I don't believe this! (*To the customers*) Don't worry, you'll all get new newspapers without holes in them.

***Bazzer**, **Yakki** and **Joe** enter. They have just finished their rounds. **Mr Ali** begins to hand out newspapers to the customers.*

Yakki	You're very busy this morning, Mr Ali.

Mr Ali ignores the boys.

Bazzer   Sorry, we're a bit late arriving back, we got held up.

Mr Ali   (*Snapping*) Can't you see I'm busy?

Yakki   Flippin' 'eck! Come on, you two, I want to look at those pictures
                    you cut out, Joe.

Joe   Yeah, they're brill! Look at this one . . .

*Joe shows Bazzer and Yakki a picture. Mr
Ali looks up and sees them looking at it.*

Bazzer   What a beauty! Where do you stick them up?

Joe   In my locker at school. Mum doesn't like me sticking them up on
                    my bedroom wall.

Mr Ali   What's that you've got, Joe?

Joe puts the picture away.

Joe   Nothing, Mr Ali. It's not important.

*Joe, Yakki and Bazzer go out of the shop into
the back room. Mr Ali begins to hand over the
papers more quickly to the customers.*

Mr Ali   Sorry Mr Hall. Sorry, Mr Watts. No, it won't happen again.

Mr Hall   I should think not. The morning paper's not the same when it's full
                    of holes.

Mr Ali   I know it isn't. Sorry, gentlemen, but I think I've just solved the
                    mystery of the missing pages. It won't happen again, I promise you.
                    (*Under his breath*) Just wait. (*He looks towards the back room*) You
                    three are for it!

· ·

Scene 3

The back room of the shop. The girls are sitting around talking.

Terry   Same again tomorrow?

Caf   Yeah. Definitely!

Tealeaf   It's far more fun than nicking!

Yakki, Joe and Bazzer enter.

Sharon   Shh! It's Yakki.

Yakki   What's that about me?

Sharon   Nothing.

Caf   Yeah, nothing for you.

Yakki   I just heard my name mentioned.

Terry   We were talking *about* you, not *to* you.

Caf   So mind your own business.

DG and Shammy enter.

Shammy   Why's Ali giving out newspapers?

Bazzer   'Cos he's a newsagent. It's his job, dodo!

Shammy   Dodo yourself. He's giving them away. He's not charging for them.

Yakki   He must have gone daft.

DG   He's always been daft.

Caf   Watch it, DG.

Shammy   He's giving copies to people who have already had them. I saw Mr Murphy getting a paper and I'd already delivered one to him.

Mr Ali storms in.

Mr Ali	Right, you three. (*He points at Bazzer, Joe and Yakki*) What have you been up to?
Bazzer	What?
Joe	Hey?
Yakki	What are you on about?
Mr Ali	Don't play the innocent with me. I heard you talking . . .
Yakki	What about?
Mr Ali	Cutting up newspapers. I've just had several customers in this morning, bringing back the newspapers *you* delivered.
Yakki	Why?
Mr Ali	Because somebody has cut out certain pictures from the papers before they delivered them.
Bazzer	What pictures?
Mr Ali	The pin-ups! The Page Threes!
Caf	(*To the boys*) You perverts.
Terry	Disgusting!
Yakki	It's not me!
Bazzer	I wouldn't do that!
DG	I haven't done that!
Joe	I haven't either!
Bazzer	Why do you think it was us? Maybe some rats ate the papers. I saw a film about it once . . .
Mr Ali	Rats do not use scissors, Barry. It has to be one of you lads. In fact, I just heard you talking about it, Joe.

Joe	What?
Shammy	When?
Mr Ali	As you walked through the shop. You said your mother didn't allow you to put up pictures on the wall, so you had to take them to school.
Joe	But, Mr Ali . . .
Mr Ali	That's enough. I've checked the customers and it's all of the boys' rounds that are affected. So, I've decided that I am not going to pick on just one of you, I'm going to take the money for replacement papers out of all the boys' wages.
Bazzer	That's not fair!
DG	I'm not paying . . .
Joe	I need the money. It's not me . . .
Yakki	Mr Ali, it's not fair, you can't do this.
Mr Ali	I can and I'm going to, unless the person responsible owns up. I'll let you sort it out amongst yourselves. You've got until tomorrow . . . and if this happens again . . . well, it had better not.

Mr Ali exits. There is a pause.

Caf	You dirty old men!
Terry	More like dirty young boys.
Sharon	You ought to be ashamed.
DG	(*To the boys*) Well, who was it? It wasn't me and so I'm not paying.
Bazzer	It wasn't me either.
Shammy	Nor me.
Yakki	(*Shaking his head*) Nor me.

They all turn and look at Joe. There is tension in the air.

Joe What are you all looking at me for?

DG 'Cos Ali heard you talking about cutting out pictures and your mum not allowing you to put them on the wall. So it has to be you!

Joe (*Scared*) It's not! My mum won't let me put up any pictures on the wall!

Yakki (*Suddenly realizing*) Hang on, we were talking about motorcycles.

Bazzer Yeah.

Joe That's right. I've cut out some motorcycle pictures from Yakki's motor sports mags, but Mum won't let me put them up.

DG What do you want to stick pictures of motorbikes up for?

Joe I like 'em.

DG What a wally . . .

Caf (*Threateningly*) So do I, DG.

DG Oh well, yeah, I suppose they *can* look good.

Caf Better than your Noddy wallpaper, DG.

They all laugh. **DG** *looks furious but doesn't reply.*

Shammy So if it wasn't Joe, who was it?

Rodge-ah enters holding a newspaper. It has had its pages cut.

Rodge-ah Have you seen this?

The boys look at him and then at each other.

DG It's Rodge-ah!

Rodge-ah	(*Confused*) What is?
DG	Get him!

> **Rodge-ah** *runs out of the shop chased by the boys. The girls crease up with laughter.*

Tealeaf	What a bunch of wallies.
Caf	Did you see their faces when Mr Ali was doin' them?
Tealeaf	And what about Rodge-ah? He'll get pulverized.

> *The girls burst out laughing again.*

Terry	Have you got the scissors?
Sharon	Yes, here they are. (*She gets out four pairs of scissors*)
Terry	Come on, let's cut some more of these shackles of slavery!
Caf	What?
Terry	Women unite and emancipate ourselves!

> *The others look blank.*

Tealeaf	Emani-whati?
Terry	Oh, it doesn't matter. Just cut these out now and we'll come in early to do tomorrow's papers.

> *They begin to cut out more pictures. They are so engrossed in their work that they don't notice the boys coming in.* **Rodge-ah** *is holding his nose. The other boys are fussing round him.*

Shammy	So if it wasn't Rodge-ah, who was it?

> *The girls are startled.*

Caf	Quick, hide them all!

Rodge-ah   My dose hurts!

Tealeaf   (*In a forced whisper*) Give me the scissors!

Yakki   We didn't know a customer had given you the paper.

Rodge-ah   You didn't ask!

> *The boys realize that there is something wrong.*

Yakki   What are you lot doing?

Terry   Er, nothing.

Caf   What's it to you?

DG   What have you got behind your back, Guts?

Sharon   Nothing, and don't call me Guts.

Bazzer   It's scissors!

> *The boys close in.*

Shammy   And papers!

Yakki   It's you lot! You've been cutting out the pictures.

DG   Right, I'm telling Mr Ali.

> ***Caf** leaps up and grabs DG.*

Caf   (*Threatening*) You're not going to tell anyone. Understand?

DG   (*Very scared*) Er, yeah.

Caf   And that goes for the rest of you as well.

Bazzer   But it's not fair, Caf. We're getting done.

Terry   There have to be casualties in a war and this is a war against the repression of women.

Caf	What are you on about, Terry?
Terry	(*Realizing that Caf will never understand*) Oh, it doesn't matter, Caf. Just threaten them.
Caf	Right! So, you lot, keep it shut . . . or else!

The boys all shuffle, looking scared.

Caf	(*To the girls*) Okay, you lot, let's go.

The girls pick up the pictures and go. There is a pause.

Bazzer	Flippin' 'eck!
Shammy	What are we going to do? We can't let them get away with this.
Joe	I need all of my wages for my bike.
DG	Don't worry, Joe. It's not only girls that can use scissors.
Bazzer	What do you mean?
DG	There are pages in papers that are for girls.
Bazzer	(*Catching on*) That's right, like fashion pages.
Shammy	And pop star pin-ups.
Rodge-ah	And the women's page in 'The Guardian'. My father disagrees with that . . .
DG	Shut up, Rodge-ah. There are pages for girls.
Shammy	And we can use scissors . . .
Yakki	And we can get other people into trouble.
DG	(*Nastily*) Exactly! Caf and that lot had better watch out, 'cos it's time for revenge!

• •

DIY Section

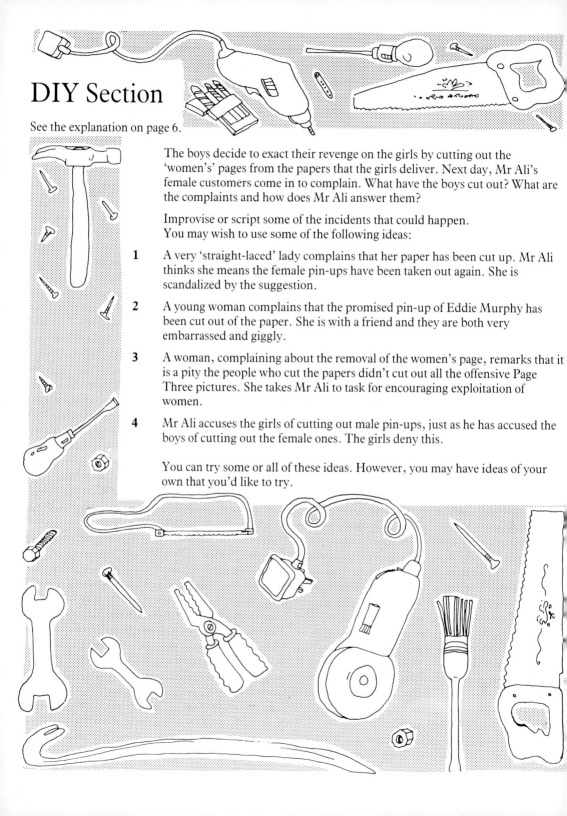

See the explanation on page 6.

The boys decide to exact their revenge on the girls by cutting out the 'women's' pages from the papers that the girls deliver. Next day, Mr Ali's female customers come in to complain. What have the boys cut out? What are the complaints and how does Mr Ali answer them?

Improvise or script some of the incidents that could happen.
You may wish to use some of the following ideas:

1   A very 'straight-laced' lady complains that her paper has been cut up. Mr Ali thinks she means the female pin-ups have been taken out again. She is scandalized by the suggestion.

2   A young woman complains that the promised pin-up of Eddie Murphy has been cut out of the paper. She is with a friend and they are both very embarrassed and giggly.

3   A woman, complaining about the removal of the women's page, remarks that it is a pity the people who cut the papers didn't cut out all the offensive Page Three pictures. She takes Mr Ali to task for encouraging exploitation of women.

4   Mr Ali accuses the girls of cutting out male pin-ups, just as he has accused the boys of cutting out the female ones. The girls deny this.

You can try some or all of these ideas. However, you may have ideas of your own that you'd like to try.

Scene 4

The back room of the paper shop. **Shammy, Yakki, Bazzer, DG, Joe,** *and* **Rodge-ah** *are sorting papers.* **Caf, Tealeaf, Terry,** *and* **Sharon** *burst in, furious.*

Caf Right, who done it?

Rodge-ah (*Correcting*) Who *did* it?

Caf I'll do you in a minute.

DG (*Innocently*) Who did what?

Terry Who cut the women's pages out of all the papers this morning?

Bazzer (*Terrible French accent*) Fear not, mammysell, ze famous defective, Ercool Parrot weel unravel zees meestery! Ah weel employ ze little grey cells . . .

Terry You ought to *be* in a little grey cell . . .

Sharon Yes, with padded walls.

Bazzer Silence! Ze great defective 'as solved ze crime! (*To Yakki*) 'Astings!

Yakki Yes, old fruit.

Bazzer Vot ees zat een your back pock-et. Mais non, eet cannot be. Eet is though, a pair ov sceesors!

Yakki Curse you, you Belgian windbag. (*He puts the scissors on the table*)

Caf (*Triumphantly*) Aha!

Shammy 'Aha' yourself. We cut the papers. How do *you* like getting done?

Sharon But why did you cut them out?

DG Because you cut Page Three out.

Terry But it's not the same.

DG Why not?

Terry	You're thick! There's a lot of difference between photos of naked women and a cookery page!
Joe	It's only a giggle.

*The girls look at him. They quieten down, but are no less threatening. **Joe** looks nervous, as well he might.*

Caf	Is it, now? And how would you like us looking at you in the nuddie, then? Terry's brought her camera.

***Terry** shows the camera.*

Joe	Leave it out.
DG	No, I reckon that's good for a laugh. Come on Joe, flex your muscles.
Joe	(*Hugging his jacket around himself*) Get lost!
Caf	Come on, Joe, it's only a giggle.
Bazzer	Yeah, come on Joe, like Mr Universe.
Shammy	More like Mr Pipecleaner.
DG	Gerrem off!

*The other boys encourage **Joe** to take off his jacket.*

Joe	I'm going.
Caf	No, you're not. Come on, get him!

*****Caf** and **Tealeaf** pounce on Joe and start to undo his jacket. Sharon looks on, uncertain. **Terry** tries to get a good picture.*

Caf	Grab his arms.
Tealeaf	Hold still!

Caf	Grab his arms!
Tealeaf	Nearly got this button – hang on Terry, don't take the picture till you see the hairs on his chest.
Sharon	He hasn't *got* any hairs on his chest.

The girls stop and stare at Sharon.

Caf	How do you know?
Sharon	He took his shirt off that hot day last summer, remember?
Terry	Oh yeah. (*Remembering*) Yuk!
Joe	Get off, ratbags!
Caf	Right, that's it, go for the trousers!
Joe	(*Blind panic*) No!

Joe bursts free of the girls. The boys jeer and catcall. Joe dives through the door with the girls in pursuit. The girls stop at the door.

Terry	There he goes, running like a headless chicken.
Caf	What a wimp! (*She turns to the boys*) Right, who's next?
Shammy	You can't scare us, Caf. You stop cutting out Page Three and we'll stop cutting out the women's pages.
Caf	Oh yeah? You'd better leave the women's pages or else we'll take re-wotsit action.
Rodge-ah	Retaliatory.
Caf	Yeah.
Bazzer	What's she on about?
Yakki	She means she'll cut something else out. Isn't that right, Caf?

Caf is not quite certain. She checks with Tealeaf and Terry. They nod.

Caf   Yeah.

DG   Like what?

Caf   Well, there's the back page, football and racin'. (*To Tealeaf and Terry*) Do you lot like football and racin'?

Terry   No.

Tealeaf   I like playing football.

Caf   Do you like reading about it?

Tealeaf   No.

Caf   Right. (*She grabs a paper from the pile*) Out it goes. (*She tears the article out*)

Shammy   Give me that! (*He snatches the paper*) Let's have a look. Here we are, fashion. That's out! (*He tears it out*)

Terry   (*Snatching the paper back*) Boxing – I hate boxing! (*Tears it out*)

Yakki   (*Snatching the paper*) 'The men in my life', by soap star Denise – we'll have that out. (*Tears it out*)

Tealeaf   (*Snatches the paper*) What about this article on the beauty contest – that's got to go, hasn't it?

Terry   Definitely. (***Tealeaf** tears it out*)

DG   (*Grabs the paper*) Right, we'll cut out everything that mentions the Royal Family.

He shares the paper out among the boys. They cut in silence for a moment. They hand the tattered remains over to Sharon. There is an uncomfortable pause.

Sharon	Well, then . . . (*Hands bits round to the girls*) . . . let's cut out all the stuff about wars and fighting 'cos it's all caused by men and done by men, and it's horrible.

The girls cut the paper. There is another pause.

Shammy	What does that leave us with?
Sharon	(*Checks*) The cartoons and the crossword.
Terry	Hang on, you can see that girl's knickers in the cartoon.
Caf	That's out then. (*Crumples the cartoon*) That just leaves the crossword.
DG	Brilliant. We can't just go out and deliver a load of crosswords.
Bazzer	My dad doesn't do the crossword. Says it's too difficult.
Rodge-ah	My father does it.
Terry	He would.
Caf	He wouldn't mind losing the rest of the paper, then, would he?
Rodge-ah	He reads the 'Financial Times', anyway.
Terry	Surprise, surprise.

Mr Ali enters, unnoticed.

Terry	Look, this is silly. We can't cut everything but the crossword. Just be sensible and leave the women's pages alone.
DG	As soon as you stop cutting up Page Three.
Caf	No chance!

She takes another paper and tears out page three.

DG	(*Snatches*) Then no women's pages . . . (*Tears*)

Caf	(*Snatches*) No football or racin' . . . (*Tears*)
Shammy	(*Snatches*) No fashion . . . (*Tears*)
Terry	(*Snatches*) No boxing . . . (*Tears*)
Yakki	(*Snatches*) No love stories . . . (*Tears*)
Tealeaf	(*Snatches*) No beauty contests . . . (*Tears*)
DG	(*Snatches*) No Princess Di . . . (*Tears*)
Sharon	(*Snatches*) No wars . . .
Mr Ali	(*Cutting in*) No jobs!

All react with shock – they hadn't known he was there.

Mr Ali	I should have realized that you lot were behind all this. What's this mess on the floor? Weren't the Page Threes and women's pages enough?
Terry	We cut Page Three out because it's degrading.
Shammy	And we cut the women's pages out because . . .
Mr Ali	. . . they cut Page Three, and so it goes on. I can imagine the rest. You can't cut everything out of the paper that might offend somebody; you'd have nothing left but the crossword.
Terry	(*Sheepishly showing the crossword*) We know.
Mr Ali	Now listen to me, this has got to stop. People want newspapers, not confetti.
Tealeaf	But papers shouldn't have those sorts of pictures in.
Mr Ali	Pauline, I don't write the papers, I only sell them.
Caf	You don't have to sell them.
Mr Ali	And you don't have to deliver them!

Caf	Eh?
Mr Ali	I have a lot of very angry and upset customers, and some of them have cancelled their papers. I pay you to deliver papers – if you don't like doing that, perhaps you'd better look for another job.

He storms out.

Shammy	Phew!
DG	(*To the girls*) That's told you lot!
Caf	(*Dangerously*) Get out before I belt you.
DG	Just going.

The boys leave.

Tealeaf	Well that's it, then.
Terry	He can't blackmail us!
Tealeaf	He can. I need this job to pay my fines.
Terry	All right then, Mr Ali, if you want to play it like this. Right, you lot, this is what we're going to do . . .

They go into a huddle.

· ·

Scene 5

*Outside the paper shop. It is early morning. **Mr Ali** enters with keys. He is about to unlock the shop. **Tealeaf** tiptoes on behind him. He hears something and turns. **Tealeaf** has hidden behind the newspaper hoarding. He shrugs, unlocks the shop and goes in. **Tealeaf** gets up and beckons to the other girls. **Sharon, Caf,** and **Terry** enter, loaded down with camping equipment – tent, sleeping bags, stove, etc.*

Sharon	(*Nervously*) He'll hear us.

Tealeaf   No he won't, he'll be in the back, counting the papers.

Caf   What if he does, anyway?

Sharon   He'll be dead mad.

Caf   Shut up, Guts.

Sharon   Well, I don't like it.

Terry   Stop moaning and give us a hand with this.

They start to set up camp.

Tealeaf   Where shall I build the fire, Caf?

Sharon   You can't light a fire on the pavement!

Terry   You can't camp on the pavement either, but we're going to.

Tealeaf   How long d'you reckon we'll have to stay here?

Terry	Dunno. Depends. Good job it's half term, we can stay a week if we have to.
Sharon	(*Horrified*) A week!
Tealeaf	Don't be pathetic, Guts – a week's nothin'. Easy-peasy.
Sharon	You call that nothing? A week camped here outside the shop all day and all night?
Tealeaf	(*Shocked*) What – nights as well?
Terry	Of course, dimbo, that's the point.
Tealeaf	What if it rains?
Sharon	Now, who's being pathetic?
Caf	That's why we've got all this gear.
Tealeaf	It's cold at night.
Terry	It's dark, too. Tell us something we don't know.
Tealeaf	But the shop isn't open at night, there's nobody to protest to.
Terry	Look, I've explained all this once . . .
Sharon	Here they come!
Caf	Ignore them.

> ***Bazzer**, **Rodge-ah**, and **Yakki*** arrive. They stop for a moment in shock, then move slowly forwards.*

Bazzer	What's going off here?
Caf	You'll find out.
Yakki	Nice spot for camping. Id-something . . .
Rodge-ah	Idyllic?

Yakki	Idiotic.

*DG and **Shammy** arrive.*

Bazzer   (*Commentary style*) And here we are with the Very Silly Mountaineering Club at their base camp, preparing for an attempt on the summit of Killymandeaded. Shortly, the assault team will set off for the top of the High Street, over the glacier outside the Glaziers, past the Tie Shop, with its dreaded bottomless cravats, then on to the gardening shop where they may catch a glimpse of the abominable Gro-bag. The expedition leader is with me now – are you prepared for this assault?

Terry   I'll assault you, in a minute.

Joe arrives.

Joe   Hey, sound! Campin'. Can I join you?

Caf   No chance. This is a women only camp.

DG   Sexist!

Terry   No, it isn't. It's a protest camp.

Shammy   A what?

Yakki   I'd protest if anyone tried to make me camp here.

Mr Ali comes out of the shop.

Mr Ali   Oh, you are here. The papers are waiting. (*He stops as he sees the camp*) What on earth is that?

Bazzer   It's not on earth, it's on the pavement. (*He collapses in a fit of giggles*)

Shammy   It's a protest camp.

Tealeaf   Like Greenhouse Common.

Rodge-ah   Green*ham* Common.

Tealeaf   Yeah, there an' all.

Caf   We're doing a virgil.

Joe   Hey, there's a lad in our class called Virgil, but he don't like camping.

Mr Ali   (*Realizing*) Do you mean a vigil?

Terry   Yes, she does.

Bazzer   Hey, I remember about Greenham Common, it was on the telly. (*The **Tigers** groan*) No, listen, it was a protest about those missiles. Loads of women went and camped around the air base where they kept the missiles . . .

DG   What did they do?

Bazzer   Well, sang songs – they had theatre groups and all that. And sometimes they tried to get through the fence, but mostly they just stayed there.

Mr Ali   A vigil. That's what it means – watching. It's a sort of protest – not noisy, not violent, just staying there, accusing, like a guilty conscience.

Terry   That's right, Mr Ali, and this camp stays here until Page Three goes.

                                        Passers-by have begun to stop and stare.

Mr Ali   I might have guessed you'd dream up something like this.

Terry   We tried cutting Page Three out and you threatened to sack us, so we're not going to do anything – just sit here.

Mr Ali   And how am I supposed to get my papers delivered?

DG   We'll deliver them, Mr Ali (*Indicating the boys*) if we get their wages as well as ours.

Terry   You strike breaker! Scab . . . scab . . . scab.

                                        The other girls join in the chant.

Mr Ali   That's enough!

Mike Input arrives.

Mike Input   This is Mike Input, roving reporter for Radio Amazing, and I've just arrived at the scene of a very unusual protest – I'm about to find out what it's all about . . . (*He looks up at the Tigers*) Oh no, you lot!

He attempts to get away, but is too late.

Terry   Hey, local radio, great! Give me the microphone, I'll tell you what it's all about.

Mike Input   No fear – last time you got hold of this mike, you got the cord round my neck. Nearly strangled me.

Terry   Come on, I'll give you an exclusive interview.

Mike Input   (*Retreating*) Good lord, is that the time? No, I have to do something safer, I'll go and report a nice quiet bank raid or something . . .

Caf   Don't let him get away.

Terry, Tealeaf and Caf tackle Mike Input. Sharon hovers. There is a brief struggle. The cord ends up between his legs.

Caf   We're setting up a virgil.

Terry   Vigil! Give it me. (*She takes the microphone from Caf*) We're setting up a vigil 'cos we don't want to deliver papers with dirty photos in them and our boss says if we don't, we'll lose our jobs, and it's exploiting women and it's not fair.

Mr Ali tries to grab the microphone, to Mike Input's immense discomfort.

Mr Ali   I didn't say I'd sack you for not delivering Page Three, I said I'd sack you if you cut my papers up again!

Terry   Well, we're staying here until they take those photos out of the paper. No more Page Three, no more Page Three . . .

The other girls join in with the chant. Mike Input manages to get the microphone back and holds up his hand for silence.

Mike Input	(*In a high squeaky voice*) Thank you. (*Clears throat and resumes in normal voice*) Thank you for that very clear explanation. Has anybody else anything to say?

Bazzer steps forward.

Mike Input	Can you shed any light on this situation, young man?
Bazzer	Yeah, well I'd just like to say . . . (*Sings 'My Way'*) And now, the end is near, and so I face the final curtain, My friends, I'll say it clear, I'll state my case, of which I'm certain . . .

*The **Tigers** realize immediately what is happening and try to stop him with shouts and by grabbing him.*

Caf	He's tryin' to sing.
Terry	Stop him!
Yakki	He's mad!

*Bazzer tries to complete the verse as the **Tigers** try to sit on him, shouting at him. He finally goes down in a tangle of arms and legs.*

Bazzer	I've lived a life that's full, I've travelled each and every byway. But more, much more than this, I did it . . . my way!

*He is finally silenced. Two **police officers** come into view.*

Tealeaf	Watch out, it's the law!

*The **Tigers** quickly pick themselves up off the floor.*

Police 1	Well, well, what have we here? A right little rogues' gallery. What is it this time, Catherine Beasley?
Caf	We're goin' to camp out here till this place stops selling Page Threes.

Police 1	Oh, are you? That's causing an obstruction, wouldn't you say, Constable?
Police 2	Oh yes, Sarge – and loitering with intent . . .
Police 1	Behaviour likely to cause a breach of the peace . . .
Police 2	Depositing litter in a public place . . .
Police 1	Not to mention illegal picketing.
Police 2	We'll think up a few more charges when we get down to the station.
Bazzer	(*Pointing to Mike Input*) You can charge him with battery!
Mike Input	Me?
Police 1	That's a serious charge, young man. Are you sure? A charge of battery?
Bazzer	Yeah, you can charge the one he's got in his tape recorder!

He roars with laughter. No one else does.

Police 1	Right, that does it. You're all nicked.
Terry	We're not doing anything, just standing here.
Police 2	There's more laws against just standing there than practically anything else you can do, isn't there, Sarge?
Terry	Well, I don't care. We're going to make a protest, and you can lock us up, but when you let us go, we'll just come back again. We'll see who gets tired first.

The girls cheer.

Police 1	(*Sighs*) Book 'em, Constable.
Mr Ali	Just a moment, Officer – may I make a suggestion? I know Terry and the others may have acted a little foolishly, but they aren't just trying to make trouble. They have a point and I don't really think that I've given them the attention they deserve.

The girls agree.

Mr Ali   If they clear all this stuff off the pavement, I'll agree to hold a proper debate in the shop, with a democratic vote, and I'll abide by the result.

Terry   Does that mean that if we vote against Page Three, you'll stop selling papers with those photos in?

Mr Ali   Exactly.

Caf   But there's six lads and only four girls. They're bound to win.

Police 1   It's either that, or a trip down the station.

Caf   Oh – Okay.

DG   She must be going soft.

Caf   If the lads help us clear it up.

DG   We never brought that stuff. Why do we have to clear it up?

Caf   (*Reasonably*) 'Cos if you don't, I'll belt you!

Yakki   That's more like the Caf we know!

They all start to clear up. The **police officers** *watch for a moment, then go.*

Mike Input   So – er – there you have it. This is Mike Input, from Radio Amazing, er, here, and wishing I were somewhere else. (*He limps off, grumbling*) Why did I have to go in for local radio? I could have been a lion tamer, or a deep-sea diver, something safe, quiet, my mother tried to warn me, I wouldn't listen though . . .

· ·

Scene 6

The back room of the paper shop. It has been set out as a debating chamber. The boys and the girls face each other. They are sitting on tables and bundles of newspapers. **Mr Ali** *is sitting in the middle. He has a tea chest beside him. He bangs it with a plimsoll in place of a gavel. The boys are chanting to the tune of 'Amazing Grace'. The girls are trying to drown them out.* **Mr Ali** *bangs the tea chest to try and restore order.*

Boys   Page Three, Page Three, Page Three, Page Three!

Girls   Page Three out, Page Three out, Page Three out!

Mr Ali   Order! Order!

Bazzer   A pint of coke and a bag of crisps!

> *He guffaws with laughter. The girls boo him and the boys scrag him.*

Mr Ali   If that is the most sensible contribution you have to make, Barry, you'd better leave.

> *The girls cheer.*

DG   Oh no you don't! We need him here so that he can vote the right way!

Caf   Your way, you mean!

DG   That's what I said.

> *More shouting and banging.*

Mr Ali   That's enough. We are going to hold this debate in a civilized manner. Here . . . (*He holds up a battered cap*) . . . is a hat. Apart from the chairman . . .

Terry   Chair*person*.

> **Mr Ali** *glares at her. She looks puzzled, then holds out her hand for the hat. He passes it to her.*

Terry	Chairperson . . .

The boys groan.

Mr Ali	Thank you, Terry, I stand corrected. Apart from the chairperson, which is me, the only person allowed to speak is the one holding the hat. When everyone has made their point, there will be a vote. Everybody will vote for a ban on Page Three, or against it. In the event of a tie, I will have the casting vote. All clear?

Caf	And if . . .

*Mr Ali glares at her. She hesitates. **Terry** passes her the hat.*

And if the vote's against Page Threes, you won't sell them any more?

Mr Ali	You have my word. But you must understand, this is a very serious business. I don't like Page Threes myself, but if I refuse to sell them, many of my customers will go elsewhere, and some of you may lose your jobs. My business will suffer as well. It isn't a step to be taken lightly.

*The **Tigers** mutter amongst themselves, then nod in agreement.*

Mr Ali	Then we'll start. Catherine has the hat, so perhaps she should begin.

Caf	Oh, er, well, I think . . . (*She is stumped. She passes the hat to Terry*)

The boys catcall.

Terry	Page Three photos just show women as sex objects. It is a shameless exploitation of women!

DG	I bet you can't spell it!

Terry	You haven't got the hat, so shut up.

***Shammy** waves to be given the hat.*

Terry	It's reinforcing stereotypes of women as second-class citizens! (*She throws the hat at Shammy.*)

Shammy	I bet you don't know half of what all that means! You're just saying what your mum says.
Terry	That's not true!
Mr Ali	Shamir has the hat, Terry.
Shammy	You haven't thought about this yourself, you just want to cause trouble and get yourself noticed.

> **Shammy** *throws the hat at Joe. He looks blankly at it.*

Joe	What's this?
Shammy	Haven't you been listening?
Joe	No, I've been reading 'Motorcycle News'.

> **Bazzer** *cuffs Joe. The girls jeer.* **Rodge-ah** *picks up the hat.*

Rodge-ah	Ladies and Gentlemen . . .

> *He is howled down by both sides.* **Mr Ali** *bangs furiously on the tea chest.*

Mr Ali	Carry on, Roger. You have the hat.
Rodge-ah	All I wanted to say is that there is no conclusive proof that these pictures cause more attacks on women . . .
Terry	(*Shouting*) And there's no proof that they don't, either!

> **DG** *grabs the hat.*

DG	What's wrong with looking at pictures like that? My dad looks at Page Three every day and he doesn't go around attacking women!

> *There is uproar.* **Tealeaf** *demands the hat. Reluctantly,* **DG** *passes it to her.*

Tealeaf	'Course, not everyone who reads Page Three goes round attacking women, just like not everyone who smokes gets cancer. It doesn't mean that it's safe, or a good thing.
Bazzer	What about the models?
Mr Ali	Wait for the hat, Barry.

The hat is passed across.

Bazzer	If it's so terrible, why do the girls in the pictures let themselves be photographed? They don't have to do it.

The hat is passed back to Tealeaf.

Tealeaf	Some of the girls are only a bit older than us. The papers promise them that they'll be rich and famous and earn loads of money. Some of 'em are skint, some of 'em are desperate . . .
Terry	And some don't think!
Shammy	And some of them agree with us!

__Mr Ali__ bangs the plimsoll. __Shammy__ waits for the hat.

Shammy	It's true, a lot of girls aren't bothered about Page Threes, so why are you moaning?
Caf	(*Grabbing the hat*) Most people aren't bothered about most things, but they should be and somebody's got to do something and . . . (*Her inspiration runs out. She thrusts the hat at Terry*)
Terry	That's right, people aren't bothered because they don't think. We should make them think about Page Threes. Little kids read the papers and giggle and laugh about Page Threes. And all they can see is that a woman is a sex object and not a real person who thinks. But it's those people in the photos who aren't real, 'cos real people wear clothes and they don't always smile and look inviting. Women are people, not dolls. We want respect!

__Terry__ furiously throws the hat to the ground.
__Yakki__ picks it up.

Yakki	I agree with most of what Terry and the girls are saying.

The boys howl in protest.

DG	Traitor!
Shammy	Get lost!
Yakki	Well, it's true, anyone can read them and look at the pictures. How would you like it if you saw some little kid sniggering over a picture of *your* sister? I know I wouldn't like it.
DG	Then don't look.
Yakki	That's no answer, you can't avoid them.
DG	We'll get you later.
Yakki	Will you? Well, that's what I don't like – being told what to do. (*He points at the boys*) I don't like you telling me what I should say in this debate.

*The girls cheer. **Yakki** turns to them.*

Yakki	And I don't like you telling me what I can and can't read, either. Because when you start thinking you know what's best for people to hear, read or look at, you might start with Page Three, but where does it end? Like yesterday, all that was left was the crossword.

*The boys sort of agree. There is a pause.
Hesitantly, **Sharon** takes the hat from Yakki.*

Sharon	I sort of agree with what Yakki says, because it's like what we did in school on censorship and dictators and secret police, and people not being allowed to read what they want. I think we should read what we want, and you can't tell people what they should think. I understand all that, only, I get frightened.
DG	What are you on about?
Yakki	Shut up, DG, let her speak, she's got the hat.

Sharon
In the winter when it's dark and I have to do my round, I think there's someone waiting for me, or when I'm walking down the alley by the railway, or I hear footsteps behind me in a street, I get frightened. I can get used to it for a bit, but then I read in the papers about someone getting attacked or murdered and then I get worried again.

There is a long pause. **Sharon** *looks at the others and then at Mr Ali.*

Mr Ali
Carry on, Sharon.

Sharon
I wonder if the man up the road, is he just walking his dog or has he got a knife? And if he says hello to me, is he being polite or is he thinking about Page Three girls? And it shouldn't be like that! I shouldn't be frightened to go out on the streets. I don't want to tell boys what they should read, but I don't want to be frightened any more . . .

There is a long and uncomfortable silence.

Mr Ali
Does anyone else have anything to say?

There is silence.

Mr Ali
Then I propose that we move to a vote. All those in favour of a ban on Page Three, raise your hands now.

The girls' hands shoot up. After a slight pause, **Yakki** *raises his hand. The girls celebrate, the boys groan and mutter.*

Mr Ali
Those against?

DG, **Shammy** *and* **Bazzer** *raise their hands.* **DG** *nudges* **Joe**, *who raises his hand. Only* **Rodge-ah** *has not voted. The girls encourage him not to vote.* **DG** *glares and makes a fist at him.* **Rodge-ah** *slowly raises his hand. The girls sigh.*

Mr Ali
The vote is tied, five all. That leaves the chairperson with the casting vote.

Terry	(*Bitterly*) Chair*man*.

*Mr Ali looks at her enquiringly. **Sharon** offers Terry the hat. Impatiently she pushes it away.*

Terry	You're a male, we know what your vote will be.
Mr Ali	Yakki's also a male, but he voted with you.

***Terry** sulks, **Mr Ali** thinks.*

Mr Ali	My vote is against.

*The girls groan, **Terry** snorts in disgust. **Mr Ali** turns to the girls.*

Mr Ali	I am sorry Terry, I'm sorry to all of you. I was very impressed by your arguments, and very moved by what Sharon had to say, but in the end, I have to ask – who am I to decide what is good for other people? If you take away the right of people to see and hear and read and think and say what they wish, you are taking away a very important basic freedom – and I think in the end, that might be a lot more dangerous than continuing to sell papers with Page Three girls in. The motion for a ban on Page Three is therefore defeated, six to five.

*The girls look dejected. **Rodge-ah** looks uncomfortable. **Joe** looks blank. **Bazzer** and **Shammy** look as if they expected victory to be a lot more fun. Only **DG** punches the air in triumph.*

DG	Yeah! 'Ere we go, 'ere we go, 'ere we go . . .

He stops as everyone, including the boys, looks at him with disgust.

Mr Ali	(*To DG*) Don't think this is a victory. Nobody wins, except the newspaper publishers, and even they don't in the end. They have wives and daughters who probably feel like Sharon. Perhaps if people had the sense to stop buying papers with pin-ups, I wouldn't need to give you these.

Mr Ali reaches into a box and produces the attack alarms. He gives each of the Tigers an alarm.

Mr Ali   I can't make it happen, though. People must be free to decide for themselves. All we can hope for is that they make the right choice. I hope you won't need to use the alarms . . .

Mr Ali puts the box on the tea chest and goes back into the shop. The Tigers leave, gradually. Caf consoles Terry and Tealeaf. Yakki watches them go, makes to say something to Shammy and Bazzer but thinks better of it and leaves. Joe yawns, Bazzer shrugs and leaves with Shammy and Rodge-ah following. Only DG and Sharon are left.

DG   Wimps!

He picks up a paper from the pile and turns to page three.

DG   (*To Sharon, challenging*) Good one today, Guts.

Sharon stares at him in disgust. She holds the alarm up to DG's head and turns it on. DG drops the paper and holds his ears in pain. Blackout.

· ·

a *Paper* *W*ar

The Characters
· · · · · · · · · · · · · · · · · ·

Caf **DG** **Shammy** **Sharon** **Kawasaki Joe** **Rodge-ah** **Bazzer** **Tealeaf** **Yakki-da** **'10p' Terry**	*The 'Paper Tigers'*
Mr Ali	*The Tigers' employer: owner of the paper shop*
Big Mal **Meltin' Ice Cream** **Spanner** **Psycho**	*formerly of Eggie Harris' gang, now delivering papers for Transglobal News*
Ms Anne Thrope	*manager of the Transglobal News shop*
Voice	*on Transglobal News tape*
Mrs Matthews	*a regular customer of Mr Ali's*
A Customer	*who enters Terry's competition*
Mrs Roberts	*owner of the 'Greasy Spoon' café*

Scene 1

The back room of the paper shop. **Bazzer** *looks in through the door and is relieved to find there is no one there. He enters, beckoning Yakki.* **Bazzer** *is carrying a sports bag. He takes out of it a diver's mask and a water pistol. He gives the pistol to Yakki.*

Bazzer   Come on then, quick, before the rest get here.

Yakki   Why?

Bazzer reaches into the bag and pulls out a black bin liner. He puts it on and struggles to get his head through a hole in the bottom of it.

Bazzer   'Cos if anyone sees me, they might think I'm mad.

Yakki   You are mad.

Bazzer   (*Putting on the mask and pulling a snorkel out of the bag*) Just get on with it, okay?

Bazzer gives Yakki the water pistol, puts the mouthpiece of the snorkel in his mouth and stands braced.

Yakki   Ready?

Bazzer   (*Through the snorkel*) Og corg oib reggy.

Yakki   What?

Bazzer   (*Takes the snorkel out of his mouth*) I said, 'Of course I'm ready'.

Yakki squirts water into Bazzer's face.

Bazzer   Urgh! Gerroff you twit, not yet!

Yakki   You said you were ready.

Bazzer   Look. I'll say 'ready' and then I'll put the tube back in my mouth, and then you squirt me, okay?

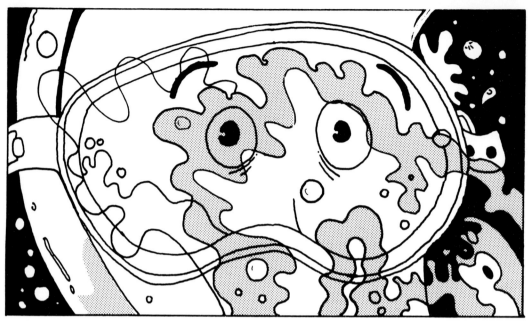

Yakki   If you say so.

Bazzer   Ready!

> *He puts the snorkel back into his mouth and* **Yakki** *squirts him repeatedly.* **Caf** *and* **Tealeaf** *come in. They stand open-mouthed.*

Caf   What's going on here?

> **Bazzer** *whips round and snatches off the mask and snorkel, trying unsuccessfully to hide them behind his back.*

Bazzer   Nothing, Caf.

Caf   Nothin'? (*To Yakki*) Well?

Yakki   There's a perfectly simple explanation.

Caf   What is it?

Yakki   (*Pointing at Bazzer*) He's mad.

Bazzer	I'm not! I was testing this mask and snorkel . . .
Caf	Testing?

Rodge-ah comes in and watches with interest.

Bazzer	They're starting a new sub-aqua club at the baths.
Caf	Come again?
Rodge-ah	Underwater swimming.
Tealeaf	Are you sure they didn't say a sub-human club?
Bazzer	This stuff is what divers wear, but it's my dad's and dead old. So I was getting Yakki to squirt water at me to see if it's still waterproof.
Tealeaf	He's demented . . .
Caf	Eh?
Rodge-ah	Round the twist . . .
Yakki	Off his trolley . . .
Tealeaf	Stark ravin' bonkers!
Caf	Belt up! You mean he's mad? (*They nod*) Well, we know that. (*To Bazzer*) Is it?
Bazzer	What?
Caf	Waterproof, dummy!
Bazzer	Well, I dunno, we hadn't finished testing it yet.
Caf	Go on, then.
Bazzer	Er, not now, Caf, I'd feel like a wally.
Caf	You are a wally. Test it!
Yakki	Come on, Bazzer.

*Bazzer puts on the mask. **Yakki** squirts him.
DG, **Shammy**, and **Joe** appear.*

DG   What's happening?

Tealeaf   It's Bazzer, he's daft.

Shammy   Tell me something I don't know.

Caf   (*To Bazzer*) Is it leaking?

Bazzer   Goad dink cho.

Caf   What?

Bazzer   (*Removes snorkel*) Don't think so.

DG   He's testing the mask, is he? Hey, Ali was cleaning the shop
                  window this morning. I'll go and see if the bucket's still there. (*He
                  goes into the shop*)

Bazzer   Hey, no, it's okay!

Tealeaf   Grab him!

*The **Tigers** grab **Bazzer**, who protests. **DG**
comes back with the bucket.*

DG   Now for a real test. Stick his head in this.

Bazzer   No, gerroff!

Shammy   Here we go! (*Putting on a bad German accent*) Ready, Herr
                  Unterseebootfurher Yakki?

Yakki   (*German*) Ya vol!

Shammy   Up periscope! (*He sticks the snorkel into Bazzer's mouth*) Dive, dive,
                  dive!

*Tealeaf makes a klaxon noise. **Bazzer** is
lifted upside down. Just as his head is about to
be immersed in the water, **Mr Ali** comes in.*

Mr Ali	What on earth! Let Barry go immediately and stop messing about. You can't put his head in the bucket, he'd need a bath before he did his round. What are you trying to do?

*The **Tigers** all try to explain at once.*

Mr Ali	Quiet! I don't think I really want to hear about it. Now, there's something I want to tell you. Are we all here?
Caf	(*Checking*) I can't see Terry.
DG	Or Guts.
Mr Ali	(*Checking his watch*) I'll see if they're coming. Check your bags please.

> ***Mr Ali** goes back into the shop. **Bazzer** takes off his snorkelling equipment. The others check their bags.*

Yakki	Hey, I keep meaning to ask, why do you call Sharon 'Guts'?
Joe	What d'you mean?
Yakki	Well, 'Guts' means fat, doesn't it? And she isn't fat.
Tealeaf	She was, though. A couple of years ago, she was massive. Then we didn't see her for ages, then she went into hospital for a bit, and when she came out she was dead thin. Weird.

***Terry** bursts in.*

DG	Ali's looking for you.
Terry	He's found me! Listen . . .
Caf	Is Guts with you?

***Mr Ali** comes in.*

Terry	No, I was round there yesterday, she's sick.
Mr Ali	Sharon's sick? Then you'll have to do her round until I can find someone to cover.

*The **Tigers** groan.*

Mr Ali   It's no use complaining. I'll sort her bag out in a moment, but first . . .

> ***Big Mal** comes in followed by **Spanner**, **Psycho**, and **Meltin' Ice Cream**. They look very pleased with themselves. The **Tigers** look daggers at them.*

Caf   Look what the cat's dragged in.

Big Mal   Tut, tut, Caferine. Anyone would think that you were not pleased to see us.

Caf   Anyone would be right.

Psycho   Pull her head off, Mal!

Caf   You and whose Rottweiler?

Mr Ali   Catherine!

Big Mal   Psycho! Down! There is no need for fisticuffs.

Caf   What's he on about?

Rodge-ah   He doesn't want a punch up.

Caf   Then what're you doin' here, sockbreath?

Psycho   Mal, lemme give her a Chinese burn. I'll just get some petrol . . .

Big Mal   Psycho, I told you to behave!

The shop bell rings.

Mr Ali   There's someone in the shop. I don't want any fighting in here while I'm out. Right? Catherine? (*She nods*) Malcolm?

Big Mal   Just a social call, Mr Ali.

Mr Ali   See it stays that way.

He goes. **Big Mal** *opens the door for him.*

Spanner   We just thought you might be interested to know that Eggie Harris has sold up . . .

Shammy   What? Sold your paper shop?

Spanner   . . . to Transglobal News.

Terry   That's what I was going to tell you all.

Caf   Belt up, Terry! So what?

Meltin'   So, this is a real snazzy outfit. They've had all the shop front done up. We are talking seriously sharp here . . .

Tealeaf   Wow, so you've got a new shop front. Big deal. But you're still paperkids, like us.

Big Mal   I beg your pardon, Tealeaf. *You* are paperkids. *We* are newscarriers.

Tealeaf   You what?

Big Mal   Newscarriers. It's all a question of image, you see, and motivation and corporal eye-dentistry.

Spanner   (*Correcting him*) Corporate identity.

Big Mal   Yeah.

Tealeaf   I thought Bazzer was daft . . .

All the **Tigers** (*except for* **DG**) *laugh.*

Big Mal   (*Getting annoyed*) You'll be laughing on the other side of your faces when our shop gets going. We are going to close you down.

Caf   Oh yeah? How?

Big Mal   By taking over your customers, cabbage brain.

Terry   You can't do that! We've got an agreement.

Big Mal	You *had* an agreement with Eggie Harris. Now Transglobal News has taken over, all agreements are off.
Tealeaf	You try comin' into our territory and see what happens.
Big Mal	I find this attitude very disappointing, Caferine. I hope that your friends are going to be co-operative – there may be jobs for some of you in the new Transglobal News branch, if you behave.
DG	What new branch?
Spanner	The one that will open here, when Ali is put out of business.
Caf	Just try it!
Big Mal	Oh, we will, Caferine, we will!

> ***Big Mal** and his gang are about to leave. He turns round at the door.*

Big Mal	Oh yes, I nearly forgot to give you this.

> *He throws a packet to **Caf**, who catches it and peers into it suspiciously.*

Caf	What's in here?
Big Mal	Lollipops . . . for suckers!

> *They leave, laughing.*

Caf	Well?
Shammy	Mr Ali wouldn't like it.
Caf	He said no fighting in here, he never said no fighting outside. Right?
Shammy	Fair enough.

> *The **Tigers** all agree (except **DG**) and move towards the door. They are stopped by **Mr Ali** coming back in.*

Mr Ali	And where are you lot going?
Tealeaf	Oh, er, we thought we'd get on with our rounds . . .
Mr Ali	Without your bags?
Tealeaf	(*Unconvincingly*) Oh, I knew I'd forgotten something.
Mr Ali	I'm sure! You will all wait until Malcolm and his friends have left the area.

Moans of disappointment from the **Tigers**.

Caf	But, Mr Ali, have you heard?
Mr Ali	About Mr Harris selling his shop? Yes, I have. I was going to tell you all about it, but Malcolm seems to have saved me the trouble.
Shammy	He said they'd force you out of business. They can't really do that, can they?
Mr Ali	I don't know, Shamir. It's very worrying.
Caf	But how?

DG has been creeping towards the door and now makes good his escape.

Mr Ali	It's a big organization. If a large business decides it wants to get rid of a small business, it's very difficult to stop it.
Tealeaf	We'll stop it!

There is general agreement among the **Tigers**.

Mr Ali	But not by fighting. I hope we can. We'll have to wait and see. Are you all ready? Where's Derek?
Yakki	DG? He was here a minute ago.
Joe	Perhaps he went to start his round early.
Yakki	DG? Never. Anyway, he's left his bag, look.

Mr Ali	Then you'll have to cover his round as well.

Mr Ali goes.

Caf	I'll do him! What's he up to? Wait till he comes back.

Tealeaf, Terry, Rodge-ah, Shammy, and Joe pick up their bags and begin to set off. Yakki and Caf are the last to leave.

Yakki	If he comes back.
Caf	If? How do you mean?
Yakki	Did you watch him while Mal was talking?

Caf shakes her head.

Yakki	Oh well, just a hunch.

He goes. Caf stares after him, thinks, shakes her head and follows him out.

· ·

Scene 2

*The paper shop. **Mr Ali** is going through an account book, looking worried. He consults a list on rough paper, checking down the account book and every so often crossing something out. The **Tigers** (except Sharon and DG) enter as an angry bunch. They shove bits of paper at Mr Ali and complain bitterly. They are all talking at once and make no sense. **Mr Ali** tries to shut them up, with no success. **Caf** finally bangs loudly on the shop counter.*

Caf	Shut up! Quiet! I said belt up! (*They do. She turns to Mr Ali*) Mr Ali, we've been nibbled!
Terry	(*Out of the corner of her mouth*) Nobbled!
Caf	Yeah, nobbled.

Shammy	Our customers have been got at.
Terry	Mal's lot have been sneaking around our area.
Yakki	They've broken the agreement.
Caf	This means war!
Bazzer	Like in Chicago, Al Capone and Bugs Moran, the St Valentine's Day Massacre . . . Chakka, chakka, chakka. (*Fires an imaginary machine gun*)
Caf	We've got to bash 'em now, Mr Ali.
Mr Ali	I've told you all, no fighting!
Caf	But they've started it. Look at this, three people on my round have cancelled their papers.
Shammy	Five on mine.
Terry	Three on mine and two on Sharon's.

*The others join in, waving their slips. **Mr Ali** says nothing, but waves the list he has been working from. The **Tigers** quieten down.*

Rodge-ah	What's that?
Mr Ali	Customers who have cancelled their orders by phone. Seventeen so far. I was crossing them off the ledger when you came in. You'd better let me have yours.

*The **Tigers** are stunned.*

Caf	Is that all you've got to say? Don't you care?
Mr Ali	Of course I care, Catherine, but what can I do?
Caf	Fight!
Mr Ali	Are you suggesting that I go round to the Transglobal News shop and thump the manager?

Caf	(*Considers, then*) Well, that'd do for starters, yeah.

*The other **Tigers** agree.*

Mr Ali	(*Wearily*) Catherine, you'll find out that one of the worst things about growing up is that you can't solve every problem with your fists. Transglobal News are doing nothing against the law, they are simply tempting customers to order their papers from them instead of us.
Tealeaf	How, though?

*The bell rings and **Mrs Matthews** enters.*

Mr Ali	Good afternoon, Mrs Matthews, what can I do for you?
Mrs Matthews	Oh er, hello Mr Ali, now what was it, oh yes, a packet of tissues please, er . . . (*She appears ill at ease*)
Mr Ali	There you are. Anything else?
Mrs Matthews	And a packet of mints, please. (*Then, in a rush*) And would you cancel my papers from Friday?
Mr Ali	Oh? Are you going on holiday?
Mrs Matthews	(*Embarrassed*) Er, no, well, the fact is, we thought we'd try that new shop up on the Hill Estate.
Tealeaf	But, Mrs Matthews, you're on my round, I always deliver your papers on time, don't I?
Mrs Matthews	Yes, love, I never said you didn't, it's just that we thought we'd fancy a change.
Tealeaf	Mr Ali can change your paper for you.
Mrs Matthews	No, that's all right, dear.
Tealeaf	But it's not fair!
Mr Ali	Pauline! I'm sorry, Mrs Matthews, we're all a bit upset. There have been a lot of cancellations today, and we don't really understand why.

Mrs Matthews	Oh, I see. I thought you must have known. I got this through the door yesterday. (*She hands over a sheet of paper to Mr Ali. The **Tigers** crowd round to see it*)
Mr Ali	(*Reading*) 'Great opening offers! All home-delivered newspapers at 5p off marked prices. Free magazine (up to £1.50) with every week's orders placed. Only at Transglobal News! Free prize draw! Every new customer automatically qualifies for our great free competition. First prize, a holiday for two in the Bahamas. All this, and the cheapest prices in town.' Yes, I thought it would be something like this.
Mrs Matthews	So, cheaper prices and a chance of a nice holiday. We couldn't refuse an offer like that, could we?

The Tigers look daggers at her.

Mrs Matthews	Ah well, yes, I must be going. Bye. (*She exits*)

Mr Ali sighs and crosses another name out of
the book. The Tigers look at the flysheet.

Bazzer	Crikey! Look at those prices. You can't get Mars Bars that cheap anywhere in town!
Terry	They're crackers! Hey look, though, it's going to be all right!

The Tigers look quizzically at her.

Terry	I mean these prices and the competition must be costing thousands, they can't be making any money. They'll go bust and then our customers will come back.
Mr Ali	I'm afraid it's not that simple. No, they can't be making any money, but that doesn't matter – a big business can afford to lose money for longer than I can. They'll wait for *me* to go bust. Then I'll have to sell this shop to them for whatever they feel like offering, because no one else will buy it. After that, when they have no competition, they can put up their prices and make up the money they lost, and a lot more besides.
Rodge-ah	My father has told me about these sorts of takeovers.
Shammy	I get it. Clever.

Tealeaf	It's not fair.
Mr Ali	There's nothing fair about business, Pauline.
Caf	(*After thought*) You're fair.
Mr Ali	That's probably why I'm going to go bust!

Mr Ali goes. The **Tigers** *look glum.*

Rodge-ah	He's going to give up, isn't he?
Caf	He may be, but we're not!
Shammy	What a sneaky idea, competitions and all that. The sort of thing that DG would dream up.
Yakki	Speaking of him, has anyone seen him?

All shake their heads.

Yakki	Just wondering.
Bazzer	I want to lie on a sunkissed beach under rippling palm trees.

They all stare at Bazzer.

Caf	You what?
Bazzer	(*Jumps*) Oh, sorry, I was just having a go at this competition. 'I'd like to win a holiday in the Bahamas because . . .' Complete this sentence in not more than fifteen of your own words. (*He sees that the others are glaring at him*) Of course, I wasn't really going to enter . . .
Tealeaf	Traitor!
Shammy	Scrag him!
Bazzer	Hey, pack it in. Just 'cos I looked at a competition.
Caf	Competition, that's it! Leave Bazzer alone. (*They let go of Bazzer reluctantly*)

Bazzer	Cheers, Caf.
Caf	You can duff him in later.
Bazzer	Eh?
Caf	Competitions! That's how we'll get the customers back, we'll have competitions as well!
Shammy	Hey, wicked idea. 'Great Celebrity Competition! First prize, a night out with Joe . . .'
Yakki	' . . . Second prize, two nights out with Joe!'
Bazzer	I thought my jokes were old.
Terry	Caf's right. That's what all the charities do nowadays.
Yakki	Great idea, but what about the prizes?
Caf	We can think of something. I mean, we can't afford much, but you can't complain if you get something for nothing, can you?

Caf leads off the other **Tigers** *(except Yakki) discussing ideas.* **Yakki** *looks at the flysheet, looks after them, shakes his head, crumples the sheet, drop kicks it through the door and follows it out.*

. . . .

DIY Section

See the explanation on page 6.

The Tigers begin to organize competitions to win back customers. Improvise or script out some scenes of these competitions.

Try out some of these ideas, or better still, improvise your own.

1. The Tigers organize a 'Guess the Weight of the Baby' competition. They 'borrow' Bazzer's cousin. His aunt discovers what is happening and rescues the baby. Bazzer has to take the place of the baby.

2. The Tigers organize a grand competition (this could be a talent contest; a look-alike contest; a dancing competition). Everything goes wrong.

3. The Tigers organize a gurning (pulling funny faces) competition. It goes horribly wrong when they award the prize to someone who hadn't entered!

Some of the following awful prizes could be won:

- a ride in a Daimler – this turns out to be a bus ticket;
- a soft top convertible – an old pram;
- a year's supply of calendars – this is *one* calendar – last year's;
- a free model of Concorde – a paper aeroplane;
- all the banana juice you can drink – this is so horrible that no one can drink any!

What happens when the winners receive these 'wonderful' prizes?

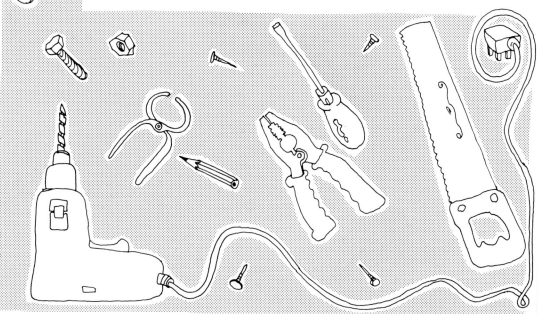

Scene 3

Outside the paper shop. **Caf, Tealeaf, Bazzer, Yakki,** *and* **Joe** *are standing about moping.*

Bazzer	(*Sarcastically*) What a great idea that was! The only competition we've been having is who can lose customers the fastest.
Caf	Shut up. It was a good idea. I thought of it.
Tealeaf	We did our best.
Yakki	I thought that one yesterday was going to work.
Joe	Which one was that?
Yakki	You know, 'Win a Time-Share'.
Joe	Oh, yeah.
Yakki	We'd probably have got a few with that, if someone hadn't twigged it meant getting a lend of Bazzer's digital watch.
Tealeaf	It wouldn't have been so bad if it hadn't been broken.
Bazzer	It was still better than Tealeaf's idea – 'Win a Year's Free Washing'.
Tealeaf	That was a brill idea!
Yakki	(*Sarcastically*) Oh yes, of course it was! Except I think people were expecting they'd get their washing done for them, not that you'd give them yours to do.
Caf	Will you stop bellyaching and let me think!
Tealeaf	Speaking of bellies, has Guts turned up yet?
Yakki	No, but there's no hurry. I reckon one of us could do all the rounds and still get home in time to see 'Blue Peter'.

Terry bursts in.

Terry	I've got it!
Bazzer	Well, don't give it to us then.

Terry   I've got a great competition.

Caf   We're sick of competitions.

Terry   But this is a real competition, we have a real prize – a hundred pounds, cash!

Caf   Eh?

Tealeaf   Where did you get a hundred quid from? Did you nick it?

Terry   No need! We can offer any prize we like as long as nobody can win it!

*The **Tigers** look at each other, puzzled.*

Joe   How d'you know nobody can win it?

Terry   Because, porridge-brain, we ask them a question that they have to get right to win the cash. But the question is so tough, nobody could possibly answer it.

Joe   I don't get it.

Terry   It's like talking to a chimpanzee. Look, remember that gig last month?

Tealeaf   You mean the Conrad Hunk concert?

Terry   Yeah. Well, all the fans invaded the stage and started tearing his clothes off and I got this!

She produces a battered training shoe from her bag. The others look incredulously at her.

Caf	So?
Terry	So, the question we ask is: 'who does this shoe belong to?'
Yakki	But that's not fair! There's no way anyone will be able to answer that!
Terry	Exactly!

> *The **Tigers** begin to smile and realize that they are on to a winner.*

Caf	Let's do it! Watch out, here's someone coming now. Let's give it a try. Go on, Terry.

> *A **customer** comes along and is stopped by Terry.*

Terry	Excuse me, I work in this paper shop and I was wondering if you'd like to place an order with us and enter our great free competition, first prize one hundred pounds cash?
Customer	Oh, yes, that sounds exciting.
Terry	(*Shocked*) You would? (*Recovering*) That's great. Would you just fill in this form?

> *As the **customer** does so, **Caf** looks down the street.*

Caf	Where's Rodge-ah?
Tealeaf	I've not seen him. What about you, Yakki?
Yakki	Nope.
Caf	This is ridiculous, what's happening to everyone? They're dropping like flies.
Terry	(*Taking the form from the customer*) Okay, now for the great competition.

> ***Bazzer** makes a trumpet fanfare. The rest glare at him. He stops.*

Terry	Now, here is your question, for one hundred pounds. Who does this shoe (*She shows it*) belong to?

> The **customer** *takes the shoe, examines it carefully and hands it back.*

Customer	Conrad Hunk.

> The **Tigers** *are thunderstruck.*

Terry	How do you know?
Customer	Because I went to the same concert and I got the other one. (*She takes an identical training shoe from a bag and shows it*)
Caf	(*To Terry*) You wally!
Terry	(*Sick as a parrot*) Ha ha! Correct, fantastic, well done! Just one more question before you can collect your hundred pounds.
Customer	What's that?
Terry	Can you run as fast as me? (*She rushes off*)
Customer	Hey! Come back! Where's my hundred pounds? (*She chases after Terry*) Come here!
Yakki	Nice idea of Terry's.
Mr Ali	(*Coming out of the shop*) Where is everybody?
Tealeaf	We're all there is, Mr Ali.
Mr Ali	Well, I suppose I can't blame the others. We're losing customers by the hour. I suppose I'd better give up now, while I still have some bargaining power left.
Caf	You can't do that! (*Desperately*) We'll work for no pay.
Mr Ali	(*Moved by this*) Thank you. It's a very kind offer, but it wouldn't be fair. Look, I'll keep going and paying you for as long as I can. Maybe something will turn up. (*He shakes his head and goes back into the shop*)

Tealeaf	Have you gone daft? Work for no pay?
Caf	He's been good to us. You know he has. He's all right.
Yakki	He can't go on much longer, though. Hey, what's this?

> *Rodge-ah staggers in. He is bruised. His clothes are ripped and dirty.*

Joe	What's happened to him?
Caf	Probably had a fight with a cat.
Tealeaf	Have you been fighting?
Rodge-ah	They grabbed me!
Yakki	Who?
Rodge-ah	Big Mal and his gang. They emptied my bag and tore my papers up, look. (*He shows that his bag is full of newspaper confetti*) Then they called me names and dragged me round and then . . . and then . . .
Caf	Yeah, what? What then?
Rodge-ah	They made me eat the front page of 'The Sporty'! And my father was right – it *is* tasteless!
Caf	That's it! They've gone too far! This time it's personal. They want a punch up, they can have one!
Yakki	But Mr Ali said . . .
Caf	I know what he said! He's wrong, though. Sometimes you gotta fight for somethin' you believe in.
Bazzer	You sound just like John Wayne!
Caf	We'll spy out the land tonight. Tealeaf, Shammy and me. Then tomorrow . . . the showdown!

> *Caf stands looking tough. The others group round. Somewhere, the music to 'High Noon' can be heard.*

Scene 4

The back room of the Transglobal News shop. The back room is like Mr Ali's, but a 'Transglobal News' sign with its logo indicates the change of location. There are a number of large cardboard boxes near the door. We hear the voice of **Ms Anne Thrope**, *the shop manager, from offstage.*

Ms Thrope   I say, you there, ya you, remove your hands from that display! (*There is a huge crash*) Oh no! Now, look what you've done. (*The shop door crashes shut*) Come back! (*The door is opened again*) Come here!

The door to the back room opens. **Caf** *and* **Shammy** *creep in, checking to see that the room is empty.*

Caf   It's okay – there's no one here.

Shammy   Nice one by Tealeaf, good idea knocking over that display to get that toffee-nosed manageress out of the shop. Think she'll catch her?

Caf   No chance, I've seen Tealeaf's getaway before – look out, someone's coming!

They look around for somewhere to hide, then dive in amongst the boxes. The door slowly opens. **Bazzer** *comes in. He is dressed as near as he can manage to James Bond. He holds one hand inside his jacket.*

Bazzer   (*As James Bond*) All right, Blofeld, I know you're in here. Come out quietly, or the cat gets it.

He prances around with a 'sucker' dart gun, taking potshots at an imaginary cat, whilst making 'miaowing' noises.

Caf   (*Standing up in a fury*) Bazzer!

Bazzer   Well, if it isn't Miss Moneypenny! James Bond, 007, at your service, licensed to kill.

Shammy	You couldn't get a licence to walk a dog.
Caf	Watch out, there's someone else coming!

> *They dive back into the boxes, dragging*
> ***Bazzer*** *into them.* ***Tealeaf*** *creeps in.*

Tealeaf	(*Whispering*) Caf! Shammy! Are you here?

> ***Caf, Shammy*** *and* ***Bazzer*** *stand up quickly.*
> ***Tealeaf*** *jumps a mile.*

Tealeaf	God, Caf! Don't do that. What are you hidin' there for?
Caf	We thought you were from the shop!
Tealeaf	Huh! I lost her round the first bend and doubled back while she was getting her breath back. (*She notices Bazzer*) What's he doin' here?
Shammy	Going.

> *Voices are suddenly heard from the shop.*

Caf	Too late! Quick, get down, they'll be here in a minute.

> *They dive into the boxes.* ***Mal, Spanner,***
> ***Psycho, Meltin' Ice Cream*** *and* ***DG*** *march*
> *in as if they were on parade. They are followed*
> *by* ***Ms Thrope***. *They form a line and continue*
> *to march on the spot. They begin the chant in*
> *time to their marching.*

Ms Thrope	How do we stay at the top?
Mal's gang	Keep on going, till we drop!
Ms Thrope	If you want to win the race . . .
Mal's gang	Stamp on someone else's face!
Ms Thrope	If you want to make a profit . . .
Mal's gang	. . . Take from someone else's pocket!

Ms Thrope	What will put us in the clear?
Mal's gang	Buying cheap and selling dear!
Ms Thrope	The worst mistake that we can make . . .
Mal's gang	. . . Is giving a sucker an even break! 1 – 2 – 3 – 4, Shove a paper through the door. 5 – 6 – 7 – 8, Never pay the going rate. 9 – 10 – 11 – 12, Sell the stock and clear the shelves. 13 – 14 – 15 – 16, Cheat and lie, but keep your nose clean. 17 – 18 – 19 – 20, They've got nothing, we've got plenty. We're the best, We're the best, We're the best, and the best don't mess!

They sit in line, like robots. **Ms Thrope**
switches on a cassette recorder she has brought
in with her. Strident, aggressive music plays.

Caf	(*Whispering to Shammy, Tealeaf and Bazzer*) What the heck's going on?
Bazzer	I've seen this on the telly. It's called motor something.
Shammy	Motivation.
Bazzer	That's it. It's supposed to get them going – hype them up. They do it in basketball and American football.
Caf	They look like a bunch of robots.
Tealeaf	What's DG doing here?
Shammy	Yakki was right – he's gone over.
Caf	Over?
Shammy	To the other side. He's joined Mal's lot.

Caf	I'll kill him!
Shammy	Shh! They'll hear you!

The music ends. A soft, syrupy voice replaces it.

Voice	Here is this week's message from Transglobal News. All our branches report record orders. We truly value the contribution of all our newscarriers.

***Mal's gang** look sickeningly smug. **Bazzer** mimes putting his finger down his throat, retches and is cuffed by **Caf**.*

Voice	We hope that this news will inspire them to greater efforts. Here are some more helpful hints in developing a positive attitude to your work: when you awake, think about the most exciting part of your day.

***Mal** and **gang** visibly think.*

Voice	As soon as you get out of bed, stand in front of a mirror and say: 'I will make the best of my abilities today'.
Mal's gang	(*Like robots*) I will make the best of my abilities today.
Voice	Eat a healthy breakfast. A healthy body means a healthy profit.
Mal's gang	A healthy body means a healthy profit.
Voice	When you arrive at work, pause briefly before you start your round, take a good, deep breath, relax, and begin the day with a positive attitude.

***Mal** and the **gang** breathe in and look 'positive'.*

Voice	And now, your Sales Improvement Executive . . .

***Ms Thrope**'s voice comes onto the tape. There has been a gap left for this in the original tape sent out by Transglobal News.*

Ms Thrope's voice	Ms Anne Thrope . . .
Voice	. . . will test you on today's handy hints.

The tape ends with music.

Ms Thrope	(*Switching off the tape*) Now then, team, let's see how well you were listening, ya? Oh-kay. What is the first thing you say in front of the mirror, on getting out of bed?
Bazzer	Who's the gorilla in the pyjamas?
Ms Thrope	(*Wheels round*) Malcolm! That was not funny!
Big Mal	I never said that, Ms Thrope, it must have been Meltin'.
Meltin'	It wasn't me!
Ms Thrope	All right! Just pay attention, ya? Now, what is the first thing you think about when you wake up?
Tealeaf	Is my hot water bottle leaking, or have I wet the bed again?
Ms Thrope	I beg your pardon?
Spanner	Psycho said that!
Psycho	I never!
Ms Thrope	If I hear any more of this, there will be a few voluntary redundancies around here. Do you catch where my breeze is taking its course? Before you start your round, you should think . . .
Caf	. . . that Transglobal News is a load of pig muck!
Ms Thrope	Who said that?
Caf	(*Standing up*) We did!

> **Shammy, Tealeaf,** and **Bazzer** *follow her example and get up.*

Caf	Anyone want to make somethin' of it?

Big Mal	(*His 'gangster' cool is gone*) What are you doin' here?
Tealeaf	Laughin' our heads off at you lot. What a bunch of dipsticks. You really fancy yourselves, don't you?
Shammy	'I've got loadsamoney, so blow everyone else.' Your own rounds aren't enough, you want ours as well. Greedy lot, aren't you?
Spanner	You've got no business coming here.
Caf	Just returning your friendly visit, Mal. And I've got business all right. (*To DG*) Especially with you, pal.
Big Mal	(*Furious*) You'd better get out!
Shammy	Make us!

The two groups square up to each other.

Ms Thrope	Stop! I will not have fighting on the premises. You had better remove yourselves before I inform the police of your presence.
Caf	We'll settle this on the reccy. Tomorrow, half-four. Right?
Big Mal	Agreed.
Caf	(*To DG*) Say your prayers, DG. You're dead!
DG	I don't think so, Caf.

*There is a confrontation between **DG** and **Caf**. She is puzzled by his coolness and goes out, followed by **Shammy**, **Tealeaf**, and **Bazzer**. **DG** starts to laugh. **Mal** looks at him in amazement.*

• •

Scene 5

The reccy. **Caf, Shammy, Tealeaf, Yakki, Joe, Terry,** *and* **Rodge-ah** *enter. They look very grim-faced and serious.*

Caf Twenty-five past four. Are we all here?

Yakki Bazzer nipped home. He said he'd be back soon.

Caf If he's chickened out, I'll . . .

Joe S'all right, he's comin'.

Bazzer walks in, wearing a cowboy hat and an old rug cut into a poncho. He is holding a paper 'cheroot' between his teeth.

Tealeaf I don't believe it. What's he supposed to be now?

Bazzer chews his 'cheroot' moodily and gazes about him with hooded eyes.

Yakki I reckon he thinks he's Clint Eastwood.

Terry Oh yeah, the Man with No Brain.

Shammy You mean the Man with No Name.

Terry I know what I mean.

Caf walks up to Bazzer and snatches off his hat and poncho, and grabs his 'cheroot'.

Caf Now listen, drongo. I've had enough of you messin' about. This isn't some cowboy film, it's real life. Mal's gang will be here in a second and we're going to fight 'em and if someone's nose gets pushed inside out, it won't be Clint Eastwood's, it'll be yours, so it'll hurt. But we're doin' this for Mr Ali and we're not goin' to let that bunch of greedy toe-rags put him out of business, so just stop pretendin'!

Bazzer Er, okay, but I'm here, aren't I?

Caf	Just don't slow us up. We're goin' to win this punch-up, we've got to. They can chant stupid slogans until their teeth fall out, but they won't beat us, because we're the Paper Tigers.
	*The **Tigers** cheer at this rallying call.*
Yakki	Watch out. Here come the opposition.
	*__Mal's gang__ arrive. **DG** is also present, carrying a big book. The two sides square up to each other.*
Big Mal	No sign of the police to save you from a thrashing, this time, Caferine.
Caf	You'd better hope they turn up to save your lot, Mal. By the time we've finished with you, you'll have to do your rounds on crutches.
Big Mal	You're wasting time, Caferine. You're all dialogue. Let's get on with it.
Caf	*(Ignoring Mal and looking at DG)* I'm surprised at you. I thought you'd be too yellow to turn up.
DG	I'm not worried, Caf.
Caf	You should be. I hope that book you're carrying is a Bible, 'cos we can use it for your funeral.
DG	No, it's not a Bible.
Big Mal	Are you going to stand here rabbiting on all day?
Caf	Ready when you are.
	*She braces herself, but **DG** steps forward.*
DG	Just a minute, Caf.
Big Mal	DG, we're wasting time.
DG	This won't take long, Mal, and I reckon you'll find it interesting. Why are you going to fight us, Caf?

Caf   You know why.

Tealeaf   (*Shouts*) Traitor!

DG   Oh, great. Another name for the collection. Double glazing, DG, four-eyes. I bet you don't even know my proper name.

Caf   Yes, I do, it's Derek.

DG   Who told you that? Ali, I'll bet. Yes, you're good at handing out nicknames, aren't you, Caf? And so's Ali. It's him you're fighting for, isn't it? For Ali – who's good at nicknames.

Big Mal   What are you on about?

DG   Getting my own back. Revenge.

Caf   You're cracked. (*She turns her back on DG*)

DG   (*Snaps*) You listen, Caf.

                              She turns. **DG** *is calmer.*

DG   Paper Tigers, that's what he calls you. Why do you think he calls you that?

Caf   'Cos we deliver his papers and we're tough. We're strong. He reckons we're the best. Right?

DG   You reckon? Well, I looked it up the other day. In here, a dictionary, not a Bible. Where is it? Paper chips . . . paper knife . . . ah, Paper Tigers: 'People who, while appearing to be strong and fierce, are in fact cowardly and weak.'

                              DG *smiles with a self-satisfied, smug expression. There is a stunned silence.*

Caf   You're lyin'. You made that up. (*She grabs him*) Say you made that up!

DG   Read it for yourself.

*Caf grabs the dictionary and looks it up.
Reads. The other **Tigers** gather round. When
Caf looks up the expression on her face is one of
total anger.*

Caf   (*Whispering*) He was laughing at us.

Mr Ali comes running in.

Mr Ali   There you are! I thought you'd be up to something like this when I
saw you gathering outside the shop. How many times do I have to
tell you that fighting isn't the way to solve anything? Go home, all of
you. Malcolm, take your friends away too. I . . . (*He realizes the
Tigers are all staring at him*) What's the matter?

Caf   You was laughing at us. All the time.

Mr Ali   What are you talking about, Catherine?

Caf   We thought you liked us. We thought you was proud of us.

Mr Ali   But I am . . . what is all this about?

Caf   (*Thrusting the dictionary under Mr Ali's nose*) We never knew. Paper
Tigers. It's in here, what it means – look at it!

Mr Ali   What?

Caf   Cowardly. Weak. Laughing at us.

*Mr Ali looks round at their faces. Realization
dawns on him.*

Mr Ali   But . . . I never meant . . . I thought you *knew*.

*Caf struggles to hold back the tears. She turns
and strides off. **Terry** and **Rodge-ah** follow.*

Tealeaf You're a bigger traitor than DG was.

*Tealeaf goes. **Bazzer, Joe**, and **Yakki** follow.*

Shammy   I think you'd better get someone else to deliver your papers, Mr Ali.

*Shammy goes. **Mr Ali** is left with Mal's gang. He looks at DG. **DG** smiles back. **Mr Ali** looks at the dictionary, at DG, and nods slowly. He hands the dictionary to DG and leaves. **DG** shouts out in triumph.*

DG   Yeah!

*He bursts out laughing. **Mal** grabs him by the throat.*

Big Mal   You stop the row, DG. You are not a nice person.

***Big Mal** leaves, followed by **Spanner, Psycho** and **Meltin'**. **DG** watches them go. He opens the dictionary and looks something up.*

DG   Wimps. Paper Tigers.

He bursts into laughter once more.

· ·

Scene 6

*The Greasy Spoon Café. **Caf, Yakki, Bazzer, Joe, Shammy, Tealeaf**, and **Rodge-ah** are slumped round a table, moodily stirring tea and tearing chocolate wrappers into strips. There is a silence and all are looking miserable. **Mrs Roberts** comes over and clears away the empty cups. She looks at the Tigers, gives an exaggerated sigh and moves away. Finally . . .*

Shammy   Look, it's not the end of the world. Someone say something!

Yakki   We don't feel like talking, Shammy, okay?

Shammy   Forget it, then.

Mrs Roberts   (*Coming over again*) Anything else?

Bazzer   Bottle of cyanide, with the top off, please.

Mrs Roberts	We haven't got any. Coffee?
Bazzer	Drink your coffee? I'm not that desperate.
Mrs Roberts	Funny boy.

She goes.

Joe	Where's Terry?
Rodge-ah	She said she was going to see Sharon, to tell her what happened.
Caf	(*Raising herself from her depression*) Sharon?
Tealeaf	Guts.
Caf	Ah. (*Sinks back into depression*)
Rodge-ah	I don't think you should call Sharon 'Guts'.
Yakki	I don't suppose it matters much after tonight . . .
Bazzer	Yeah, but we'll still see each other at school.
Tealeaf	Won't be the same though, will it? We're all in different classes. Different forms. We'll be like anybody else.
Shammy	No more going to the shop.
Yakki	No more putting one over Mal's gang.
Bazzer	Hey, remember when . . .?
Tealeaf	Shut up, Bazzer. We're not in the mood for remember when-ing.
Bazzer	Yeah, but remember when . . . (*He sees everyone except Caf glaring at him*) . . . oh, all right.
Shammy	Who's going to ask Ali for this week's money?
Caf	(*Bitterly*) He can keep it.

There is silence.

Tealeaf	Dunno how I'm going to pay my fines now.
Joe	I've been saving for a Kwaker like my brother's. Don't suppose I'll get one now.
Yakki	What if Ali apologized to us?

> **Caf** *stares stoney-faced at him.*

Yakki	No, no, forget it.

> **Sharon** *enters followed by* **Terry***. She looks very ill, but also angry.* **Terry** *looks completely shocked.*

Shammy	Hey, Guts! Are you better, then?

> **Sharon** *doesn't answer, just stares at them.*

Sharon	(*Angrily*) Just look at you! Sitting there moping like a bunch of little kids sent home from nursery school.
Yakki	Don't you start.
Sharon	Do you know what a bunch of wallies you look?
Shammy	Terry, haven't you told her?
Terry	Of course I've told her. I told her what DG had found out, and that we'd left Ali's and she went loopy! I don't know what's up with her.
Bazzer	Maybe she's suffering from conclusions.
Rodge-ah	*De*lusions.
Bazzer	Them as well. That's it, she's delicious.
Rodge-ah	De*lirious*.
Tealeaf	(*Worried*) You reckon she is? Are you sure you're all right, Guts? You'd better lie down.
Sharon	Am I all right? That's a laugh. I'm fine, it's you who aren't.

Yakki	But don't you know what Ali did? Didn't Terry tell you what 'Paper Tigers' means?
Sharon	Yes, but she didn't have to, I already knew.
Caf	(*Raising herself*) You knew?
Sharon	Of course. I've always known. I thought *you* knew.
Caf	*What?*
Sharon	I thought it was pretty funny.
Caf	Funny?
Sharon	Yes. What does it matter, anyway?
Caf	What does it matter?
Sharon	Are you a parrot?

Caf is about to burst a blood vessel.

Shammy	Look, Guts, you don't get it. All the time we thought Ali liked us, he was laughing at us. He gave us that nickname.
Sharon	(*Viciously*) Nicknames, hey? I know all about nicknames. Do you want me to tell you about nicknames?
Caf	If you've got something sensible to say for a change . . .
Sharon	(*To Caf*) Why don't you shut your stupid great gob!

There is a stunned silence. No one has ever addressed Caf like this before.

Sharon	Do you remember when I was fat? You called me Guts. You still do, even though I'm thin. That was nice, wasn't it? You must have really liked me, giving me a nickname like that.
Joe	It wasn't just us . . .

Sharon	(*Ignoring him*) I really hated that nickname. You know the saying: 'Sticks and stones may break my bones, but names will never hurt me'. That's a lie! Names do hurt. I used to go cold when I heard that name. So d'you know what I did? I decided I'd be thin. I stopped eating. I did more than that even. When my mum made me eat, I'd stick my fingers down my throat and make myself sick.
Bazzer	Leave it out, Guts. I feel ill.
Sharon	What's up, Bazzer? Never seen a programme about that? It's got a name, what happened to me, what I did to myself. I couldn't stop. I made myself ill, I had to go into hospital . . .
Tealeaf	I remember that!
Sharon	. . . I still do. Every week, I have to go and see someone. I still can't stop. I have to force myself to eat, then I feel guilty, like I've murdered someone.
Shammy	What?
Sharon	Yeah, sounds stupid, doesn't it? But it's a disease. You can't catch it, you can only do it to yourself, like I did. That's why I've been off, I stopped eating for too long.
Terry	But isn't there a cure?
Sharon	Oh yeah, but less than half the people who've got it get better. So I'll probably always have it. I'll have to make myself eat to stay alive. All because I got upset by a stupid nickname.
Shammy	And you didn't even get rid of that.
Sharon	No.
Terry	(*Very upset*) I'll make sure no one ever calls you that again.
Sharon	That's not the point. The point is, you've all done what Mr Ali's done, but you didn't mean well like he did.
Caf	Mean well?

Sharon   Yes! Why are you moaning about nicknames? Do you think that DG liked the nickname you gave him? Why do you think he's gone over to Mal?

Caf   'Cos he's a traitor.

Sharon   But you didn't help him not to be, did you? What about Yakki? D'you suppose he likes his name?

Caf   He doesn't mind.

Sharon   How do you know what he likes?

Caf   (*To Yakki*) Do you?

Yakki   (*Embarrassed*) Er, well . . .

Sharon   And Rodge-ah?

Caf   That's his name!

Sharon   Not the way you say it.

Tealeaf   I like my nickname.

Joe   And me.

Sharon   Of course you do. You think your nickname fits you. Mr Ali gave us a nickname that he thought suited us, and then you found out it didn't mean what you thought it meant. Big deal! But I bet he never laughed at us. Or if he did, he didn't mean anything. He likes us too much to do that.

Caf   (*Defiantly*) Oh, yeah!

Sharon   Of course he does! Who let you keep your job when you accused him of being a drug dealer? Who didn't tell the police about the bath? Who fished Joe's brother's bike out of the canal and fixed it?

Joe   Yeah, he saved my life by doing that. My brother would've killed me!

Sharon	Who gave us a rise whenever he could and kept paying us, even when we were off sick, and gave us the alarms and stuck up for us? What's he got to do to prove that he likes us?
Caf	But he gave us that name and was laughing at us! We trusted him. He made us trust him, and yeah, I thought it was 'cos he liked us, but it wasn't, was it? He just got us to like him so he could make fools of us. Right? (*She looks around at the Tigers*) Right?

There is an uncomfortable silence.

Shammy	No, Caf. Sorry, I reckon Gu . . . Sharon's right.
Joe	I don't reckon he meant it, really.
Caf	You mean you're going crawling back?
Terry	Not crawling.
Rodge-ah	Sharon *is* right, Caf.
Caf	You're pathetic.
Tealeaf	It's not us who's being pathetic.
Caf	Watch it!
Yakki	Come on, Caf.
Bazzer	Yeah, I reckon we should go back.
Shammy	We'll go and tell him in the morning.
Sharon	Tell him now, he's in the shop. Me and Terry called in on the way here. He's doing the books – says he's going to advertise the shop for sale tomorrow.
Shammy	We'll go now, then. Are you coming, Caf?

Caf sits staring hard. She shakes her head.

Shammy	Suit yourself.

He goes, followed by the others. **Tealeaf** *stops at the door.*

Tealeaf	Come on, Caf.

There is no response. **Tealeaf** *goes.* **Caf** *lowers her head onto her arms.* **Mrs Roberts** *comes over.*

Mrs Roberts I'm shutting up in a moment. (*She sees* **Caf**'*s shoulders are shaking*) Here, are you all right?

Caf *is crying like a little child.* **Mrs Roberts** *puts her arm round her.*

Mrs Roberts (*Comforting Caf*) There, there.

. . . .

Scene 7

Outside **Mr Ali**'*s paper shop.* **Shammy, Rodge-ah, Terry, Bazzer, Yakki, Joe,** *and* **Tealeaf** *are about to set out with very slim newpaper bags.* **Mr Ali** *is watching them.*

Shammy Right, we'll get these delivered then.

Bazzer Yeah, shouldn't take long.

Mr Ali You're right there, Barry. Even without Catherine, Derek and Sharon, there's not much work to go round. But I'm very pleased you came back.

Tealeaf (*Snaps*) So why did you call us that stupid name?

Mr Ali Believe me, I wasn't laughing at you, Pauline. I never meant to insult you or hurt your feelings. I thought you liked the name.

Joe Forget it, Mr Ali.

Yakki Yeah, it doesn't matter.

Mr Ali It does to me. I'm sorry that Catherine hasn't come back.

Terry	Well, you know Caf. She'll be back. Give her a few weeks.
Mr Ali	I'm afraid I don't have a few weeks. I have to face the truth. I think this will probably be your last delivery.

> The **Tigers** protest. **Sharon** enters and they are suddenly quiet.

Sharon	Where's my bag, Mr Ali?
Terry	Go home, Sharon, you're still sick.
Sharon	I feel better. I want to work.
Tealeaf	There's no need, we can cover your round, dead easy.
Sharon	But I want to help . . . (*She begins to cry*)

> **Mr Ali** watches her helplessly. **Tealeaf** and **Terry** comfort her.

Yakki	(*To Mr Ali*) We all want to help.
Mr Ali	I know, thank you, but I'm afraid it's too late for anyone to do anything. Sharon, come into the shop and you can help me with the accounts. Come on.

> He helps Sharon into the shop. As the **Tigers** watch, **Big Mal, Spanner, Psycho**, and **DG** enter.

Shammy	(*Hard*) What do you lot want?
Big Mal	And convivial greetings to you, Shamir, as well. We were just passing through the area, so we thought we'd drop by for a quick gloat.
Psycho	Yeah, rub their faces in it, Mal.
DG	Look at the state of those bags. Ali's finished.
Terry	(*Defiantly*) No he isn't.

DG	(*Laughing*) Still sticking up for him? You're stupid. You should have got out when the going was good, like I did. Look at me now!
Tealeaf	No thanks, I don't want to be sick.
Rodge-ah	(*Brainwave*) Hang on, why aren't you out delivering your papers?
Spanner	Because our shop has given us the afternoon off.
DG	Yeah, see, that's what happens when you work for an organization like Transglobal News, and not some crummy dive.
Rodge-ah	(*Carefully*) So who's delivering your papers, then?
Spanner	How d'you mean?
Rodge-ah	Well, your customers will still want their papers. If you get time off, how do they get them?
Big Mal	(*Blustering, but worried*) Ah well, er . . . I daresay that there is a full back-up system . . .
Shammy	You look worried, Mal.
DG	Hey Mal, you don't reckon that Thrope is stitching us up?
Big Mal	Belt up! Come on, you lot, we've got better things to do than stand round here talking to these no-hopers.
Shammy	Just a minute, Mal. Leave DG here. We want to have a little word with him about various incidents.
Big Mal	Forget it. DG's with us now. Even if he is a total creep . . .
DG	What!
Big Mal	. . . He's one of us, and I'm not going to let you lot touch any of my lot.
Shammy	Come to think of it, we still owe you for Rodge-ah.
Big Mal	That was a joke.

Shammy	Rodge-ah didn't laugh. (*To Rodge-ah*) Did you?
Rodge-ah	Well . . . er, no, but there's no need to fight about it.
Shammy	(*Ignoring him*) So Mal, do you leave DG with us or do you want a fight?
Big Mal	All of us, or just you and me?
Shammy	I'm easy.
Big Mal	Right then.

> *The two sides square up.* **Rodge-ah** *runs into the shop to get Mr Ali. The fight is about to commence, when* **Caf** *runs in, breathless.*

Caf	Oi! Pack it in!
Terry	Caf!
Big Mal	If you want to join in, be my guest.
Caf	No, I don't want to fight. There's no need.

> *There is a stunned silence.*

Spanner	You, not wanting to fight! Have you gone soft?
Caf	There's no need to fight. It's all over.
DG	Yeah, she's right. Ali's finished.
Caf	No. Transglobal News is, and so are you.
Big Mal	What are you on about?
Caf	Read this. It was on the window of your shop.

> **Caf** *hands Mal a poster. He opens it out.* **Spanner, Psycho**, *and* **DG** *crowd around it.*

Big Mal	(*Reads*) 'We are moving' . . . eh?

Joe	Who's moving?

*Big Mal looks worriedly at his gang and
continues to read.*

Big Mal	(*Reading*) 'Due to our extensive ration . . . ration . . .'
DG	Rationalization.
Big Mal	Belt up! '. . . programme, Transglobal News is closing this branch.' Gordon Bennet!
Shammy	What? Give it here! (*He snatches it from Mal, who is too shocked to protest*) 'We look forward to welcoming you to our new megastore in the Glasshouse Shopping Mall, Easthampton.' That's miles away!
Bazzer	Look at the small print. 'We regret that our home delivery service will be discontinued immediately.'
Big Mal	(*Shocked*) What a carve-up.
Terry	There's more at the bottom. 'Opening on this site shortly: "Happy Feet Shoe Boutique".'
Bazzer	Hey Mal, maybe you could get jobs as 'shoescarriers'.
DG	She's made it up, I bet!
Big Mal	Yeah, that's it, you've made it up.
Caf	I don't think so. I went round to your shop to do the lot of you and I found it.
Psycho	Take us all on? You're daft!
Tealeaf	Why, Caf?
DG	(*Nastily*) I know why, so Ali would feel guilty when you were all smashed up.
Shammy	(*Viciously*) Who asked you? You're history, boy.

Meltin' Ice Cream rushes in.

Meltin'	Hey, Mal, I just saw Ms Thrope drivin' off in her car. She gave me this note to give to you.

> *Meltin'* gives Mal a note. Again the **gang** crowds round. **Mr Ali, Sharon**, and **Rodge-ah** rush out of the shop to stop the fight but are stopped dead in their tracks, when they realize there isn't one.

Big Mal	(*Reads*) 'Dear all, I hate goodbyes, so I'm off to Easthampton to run the new megastore. We've decided to stop the home deliveries as they weren't really profitable. Sorry, but business is business.' She's stitched us up!
Mr Ali	What's going on here? Roger said there was going to be a fight.
Terry	There's no need. Look at this poster. (*She hands Mr Ali the poster*)
Shammy	So it looks as though we're the only paper shop in the area!

> The **Tigers** cheer. **Mal's gang** look sick.

Mr Ali	(*Amazed*) Incredible! Yes, it seems that we are.
Terry	And that means more customers.
Yakki	So our jobs are safe!
Mr Ali	Not only safe, we'll need more people.

> The **Tigers** look at Mal's gang.

Shammy	I remember Mal saying that there would be jobs for some of us with you lot, if we co-operated.
Mr Ali	(*Catching on*) Hmmm, yes, we could do with experienced delivery people. There should be jobs for everyone.
Tealeaf	But not DG!
Mr Ali	(*Slowly*) No. On the whole, better not.
DG	You mean you'll give all these a job, even Psycho, but not me?

Mr Ali   I'm afraid not, Derek.

                  DG is shattered.

Joe   Caf found out, Mr Ali! She went up to their shop to take them all on. Awesome bottle!

Mr Ali   (*Smiles ruefully*) I'm glad to see you back, Catherine.

Caf   Yeah, well, I got bored, didn't I? (*She is secretly pleased*)

Big Mal   (*Reasserting his authority*) Right, we'd better get round to our customers, get them to order from Mr Ali.

Shammy   Just a minute Mal, you're forgetting who's in charge. (*He nods at Caf*)

Caf   (*Taken unaware*) What? Oh yes, (*Casually*) yeah, good idea, Mal. We'll do our rounds and meet back here after. Okay, Mr Ali?

Mr Ali   Okay, Caf. Perhaps Sharon and I could arrange a little party to welcome our new 'newscarriers'.

Caf   Paper Tigers, Mr Ali. We're all going to be Paper Tigers. Right, Mal?

Big Mal   (*Through clenched teeth*) Right, Caferine.

Caf   Let's go. (*To DG*) Are you still here?

DG   Come on Caf, can't you take a joke?

Caf   Yeah, I can take a joke – now. What I can't take is you. Get lost before . . . (*She shows him a fist*)

DG   You're going to be sorry about this. You haven't seen the last of me. I'm gonna get you back – the lot of you. You watch your backs, 'cos one day . . . one day . . . I'll have the lot of you.

                  *The **Tigers** advance menacingly. **DG** snorts and rushes off.*

Tealeaf   You don't think he'll do anything, do you?

Caf	No. Just forget him. Come on, we've got work to do.

*The **customer** who answered Terry's question enters.*

Customer	Excuse me, have you seen . . . (*Spots Terry*) Ah, there you are! Where's my hundred quid?
Terry	Time to go! (*She rushes off*)
Customer	Hey, come back here! (*Chases after Terry*)
Caf	Come on, let's go!

*Caf leads **Yakki**, **Bazzer**, **Rodge-ah**, **Tealeaf**, **Shammy**, and **Joe** off after the customer. They are all whooping and yelling.*

Big Mal	Anyone know what that's all about? No? Ah well, if you can't beat them . . .

***Mal's gang** chase off, yelling and whooping.*

Mr Ali	(*To Sharon*) Here we go again. (*Starting to go*) What's this about a hundred quid? (*He goes*)

***Sharon** laughs. She goes into the shop. She brings out a sign and places it on the newspaper hoarding. It says 'Business as usual'. She goes back into the shop and shuts the door. The shop bell tinkles.*

· ·

Activities

· ·

What the Authors Say

When Oxford University Press asked us to write some more plays about the
Paper Tigers, we thought for a bit, then looked at each other and said, 'We'd
better ask them.'
Bazzer said, 'Chill out! Ace! Sound, wicked, t'riffic, epic . . .' and lots more of
the same.
DG said, 'How much?'
Tealeaf said, 'Okay, I liked the first book.'
'Did you buy it, then?' we asked.
'Nah, I nicked it.'
Rodge-ah said that his father had read **Paper Tigers** and that he (the father)
thought all the children that he (Rodge-ah) was mixing with seemed to be a lot
of scruffs and that he (the father) would have to see about it. We took that as a
'yes'.
Sharon said, 'Er . . .'
Shammy and Yakki said okay, but Shammy thought that Terry should be in
this book, so we asked her.
She said yes, as long as we typed everything on recycled paper, and added that
our wallets looked very heavy and uncomfortable and perhaps she could
relieve us of any five pound notes we no longer happened to want, to help the
stray cats' home.
Joe said, 'Eh?' (He was reading *Bike* magazine, so we left him alone.)
'Depends,' said Caf. 'You never let me beat up Mal in the last book. There
were always coppers interferin'.'
'Sorry,' we muttered.
'Yeah, well you can do it if you write, "So Caf and the Tigers go round to
Eggie's place while the coppers are all watching *Neighbours* and duff over Mal's
gang somethin' wicked," okay?'
We said we'd think about it.
That made it unanimous (more or less), so we put it to Mr Ali.
'*Another* book?' he asked, shaken.
'Yes,' we said.
'My mother starts giggling every time she sees me,' he protested, 'and my
uncles usually make jokes about custard powder, or baths, or fishing for bikes
in canals. And you want to write *another* book?'
He gave a sigh and turned away to serve a customer, and since he hadn't
actually said 'No', we took that as a 'yes', too.

Of course, the most convenient thing about people who exist only in our
minds, is that they usually do agree to do what we want them to do. Also, they
don't move away unexpectedly, and forget to write. We always know what
they are going to do next, or at least we know what they are going to do before
they do, which is very handy. And because they are in our heads, we know
where to find them.
Best of all, unlike other people who have arguments and spring cleaning and

chicken pox and go out shopping or to the pictures, we can visit them any time we want to.

And when you read the plays, of course, so can you.

Steve Barlow and Steve Skidmore

Understanding the Plays

When we wrote these plays, we had to decide three things:

1   Who would be the characters in the play?
2   What would they say to each other?
3   What would happen to them?

We obviously wanted to make the plays enjoyable and fun to read and act out, but we also wanted to make you think about the way the characters behave.

We have done this by putting clues into each play which will help you to understand why the characters behave as they do. When you read these plays, you will have to be detectives. You will have to find these clues and be ready to produce them as evidence to back up your ideas about the play and the characters.

To help you in your detective work, the following pages contain suggestions of things you can do to explore the meaning of each play. All good detectives need methods to solve mysteries. Here are some of the methods you can use:

Improvisation   You are given a situation to work on in groups. Using your own words, you act out a scene which shows what you think about this subject. There are two main types of improvisation:

1   **Planned:** in which you are given time to prepare your work by talking with your friends and trying out your ideas. When you have practised your work and are satisfied with it, you show it to other people.
2   **Instant:** in which you are given a character and a situation, but you are not given any time to prepare. You must start the improvisation straight away.

Role Play   A situation is chosen, and every member of the group must pretend to be a character in that situation and act as that character would. For example, in a role play about a circus, members of the group would take on the roles of all the different characters you might see there: clowns, trapeze artists, acrobats, lion tamer, tightrope walker, etc.

Still Images

A still image is like a photograph. Any number of people may be in the image. A situation is chosen and the group must produce a frozen picture as if they had been captured on film by a photographer. You may wish to choose just one image, or use a series of images to tell a story.

Thought Banding

This helps us to understand what the characters in a still image are thinking. In turn, each member of the group says what their character was thinking at the moment the 'photograph' was taken.

Hot Seating

When a member of the group has played a character in an improvisation, a role play, or a written play, they can be put in the 'hot seat'. Decide which character you wish to question, and then choose a member of your group to sit in the 'hot seat', facing the rest of the group. The rest of the group asks the person in the 'hot seat' questions and this person then gives answers as if they were that character.

Brainstorming

This can be done in small groups (using pen and paper) or as a full class (using a chalkboard or marker board, flipchart, etc). One member of the group is chosen to write down any comments the group makes about a play or a chosen topic. These can be single words or short sentences. Write down everything that is said, no matter how silly it may sound. After a few minutes, look at the paper or board, and talk about what you have said.

Terry's Tramp

Character

Terry is a new character. As a group, brainstorm the words you would use to describe her.

Discuss

At the beginning of the play, Terry seems to have a kind heart because she is always collecting for charity. However, at the end of the play she decides that she has been mean and selfish.

Is Terry kind or selfish? Break up into small groups to discuss this. You must find evidence in the play to back up your thoughts. Choose incidents or lines from the play to help you do this and write these down so that you can remember them. When you have collected your evidence, choose one person from the group to present your findings to the rest of the class.

What words would you use to describe Mr Wibble, Mrs Prendergast and Mike Input? Back up your ideas with evidence from the play.

Theme: The Homeless

Discuss

Cardboard City and the question of homelessness is frequently front page news. Sometimes homeless people are called 'tramps' or 'down-and-outs'. Have you ever seen any 'down-and-outs' in your city, town or village? Who are they and how did they come to be 'down-and-outs'? In order to help your discussion, find some facts and figures about people who are homeless. You will find information in books, newspapers and magazines. Your local library will be able to help you.

Write

Try to imagine that you are a homeless person in a city. **Brainstorm** suggestions of where you might go to find a place to sleep. Make a list of these ideas.

Discuss

If a 'down-and-out' approached you in the street and asked for money, how would you feel? Would you be frightened, embarrassed, or angry? Would you give them the money?

Discuss

How are the homeless and 'down-and-outs' treated by other people? What are our views about such people? Could we do more for them? Should we? Talk about your views with the rest of your group.

A Newspaper Article

Write

You are a reporter who covers the Tigers' protest outside the DSS office. Write a front page newspaper article describing the protest. Include descriptions of the demonstration and make up interviews with several of the characters. You can use **role play** or **hot seating** to question the characters. Interview:

    The Tramp
    Terry
    Mr Wibble
    Mrs Prendergast

How different are their views? Include some of the interviews in your article. Remember to pick out the most important points in order to make the article interesting.

You could even photograph some of your friends as if they were some of the characters from the play, and use these photographs in the article.

Terry's Diary

Write

Imagine you are Terry. Write her diary covering the period of time when she becomes involved in trying to help the tramp. Remember to put her thoughts and feelings down. How does she feel towards the tramp at first and how does this change?

What are her thoughts about Rodge-ah? What plans might she be making? Do these work?

Try to make the diary as interesting as possible. Use the facts from the play and add your own ideas and thoughts.

Demonstrations

Talk

Use these questions to help your group talk about the subject of demonstrations.

1   Why do people hold demonstrations?
2   Do they do any good or are they just an excuse for people to make a nuisance of themselves?
3   What would you demonstrate about?
4   Most demonstrations are either *against* something ('Ban the Bomb', 'Stop the Motorway') or *for* something ('Save the Whales', 'More Pay for Nurses').

Decide on a subject that concerns you. It could be something internationally important, like the environment, or it could be something locally important or even important to your school.
Decide if you are *for* or *against* and discuss this with your group.

Charities

Terry is into 'good causes'. She likes to help charities by collecting money.
Make a list of the charities you know. Are there any causes which you think are more worth supporting than others? Are there any charities that you would not collect for or donate money to? Why not? Discuss this with the rest of the class.

Design

Then design and draw a poster for a charity or a cause. This could be anything from 'Save the Whales' to 'Comic Relief'. You might like to make up your own cause: 'Save the Teacher!' or 'Pay the Pupils!'

Research

Try to find out how charities work and what they do. You might even wish to organize your own fund raising event for the charity of your choice.

Drama Ideas

1   Hot Seating

Hot seat Rodge-ah. Try to find out what makes him change his mind about the tramp.
Hot seat Terry. Find out what has caused her to feel ashamed of herself by the end of the play.

2   Improvisation

Work in pairs.
Role A is a person your own age.
Role B is a 'down-and-out'.
Situation: the 'down-and-out' approaches the other person to ask them for money. Act out this instant improvisation.
After you have finished the improvisation, discuss how it went. Try to answer these questions:
   How did you react to the 'down-and-out'?
   How did the 'down-and-out' feel about asking for money?
Reverse the roles so that the person playing the 'down-and-out' now plays the part of the young person and vice versa.

Work in pairs again. This time both of you are 'down-and-outs'. There is one park bench and both of you want it for your bed. How do you decide who has it? Play this scene.

3   Still Images

In small groups, create a still image of a group of homeless people. This could be set around a fire on a piece of waste ground, or on a street late at night. It is cold, and raining. There is very little shelter. What are you thinking about? Are you remembering better times or looking forward to better times to come? Form this still image and thought band each person. After you have done this, discuss your thoughts with the rest of the group.

4   Role Play

This is a whole group role play, in which all the group simultaneously take on the roles of different characters.

Set up your classroom or studio as the dining room of a hostel for 'down-and-outs'. There should be tables, chairs and a kitchen area. There could be a sleeping area as well.

Choose some people to be the workers at the hostel. It is their job to run the hostel, providing shelter and food for the homeless people who visit it for a meal and a bed. The rest of the group take on the roles of 'down-and-outs'.

In small groups, use the hot seating technique to help you create your character.

Begin the role play when the homeless are arriving for an evening meal.
How do the staff act towards them?
How do the homeless react to the staff and to each other?
After a period of time, stop the role play and discuss what happened and how you felt as the character you were playing.

After you have done this, continue the role play. This time, however, one of the helpers announces that there is not enough room for everyone to stop for the night. Everyone playing the role of a homeless person has to give a convincing reason why they should be given a bed for the night. The workers have to decide who is going to stay, basing their decision on the arguments presented by the homeless.

One of Our Pages is Missing

Character

Write

Make a list of all the male Tigers.

Next to each name, write down as many reasons as you can think of why that character thinks Page Three pin-ups should continue to be published.

Do the same for all the girls, giving reasons why each girl thinks Page Three pin-ups should not be published.

Talk

Talk about the characters. Do all the characters give the reasons you would expect from what you know of them? Are there any surprises? One of the characters changes their point of view on this issue. Who is this? What causes that character's change of mind?

Mr Ali is usually a strong character who is confident that he knows what is right. For instance, he makes Rodge-ah think twice about his attitude in **Terry's Tramp.** However, in this play, he seems less than certain about what he should do. Why do you think this is?

Theme 1: Exploitation of Women

Think

Both the boys and Mr Cook (the customer who complains first) are embarrassed that they have been found out looking at, or wanting to look at, Page Three pin-ups. If the boys are right and there is nothing wrong with looking at such photographs, why are they ashamed?

Ms Payne calls Mr Cook a 'dirty old man'. Is she being fair?

Think

The girls think that Page Three type photographs exploit women. The boys disagree. What do you think? Read the arguments both sides give in the play. Think of other arguments for both sides which nobody mentions in the play.

Discuss

Questions to consider in your discussion:

Are there any ways (besides newspaper photos) in which women are exploited in your view? Make notes under headings: Magazines, TV, Film, etc.

If you can think of other ways in which women are exploited, why is it that women allow it to go on?

Why do you think Page Three models choose to earn their money this way?

Is there any way in which Page Three type photographs actually exploit *men* and affect their attitudes?

Can you think of any other ways in which men are exploited?

Do you think there is a link between Page Three type photographs and violent attacks on women?

Theme 2: Censorship

Discuss

What is censorship? **Brainstorm**, then discuss your ideas.
Why do you think censorship exists?
Brainstorm as many examples of censorship as you can think of.

Write

Make a list of these using the following headings:
To protect children
To protect adults
Security reasons
Religious reasons.
Who are the people who take decisions about censoring things? Do you think they should have the right to do this?

Discuss

Mr Ali eventually decides he has no right to decide what people should or should not read or look at in newspapers.
Do you agree with him?
Do you think censorship is generally wrong, but in some cases so important that it should be used?
Do you think there is not enough control over what newspapers are allowed to print?

Debate

After your discussion has taken place, arrange a debate on the two issues.
Set it up in the same way that the Tigers set up theirs.
Only one person may speak at a time. When everyone has said all that they wish to say, take a vote. Count the votes and announce the result.

The two motions are:
- We believe that Page Three type photographs exploit women.
- We believe that censorship should never be used.

Write a Letter

Write

Imagine that you are one of the Tigers. You are writing a letter to a friend, who lives in another town.
You are going to tell them what has happened since the girls first found the boys looking at Page Three photos.
Of course, what you write and how you explain the events will depend on which character you choose to be.
Terry's letter might begin:

Dear Julie,
      I've had a really rotten week and I'm fed up. It all started when we caught those filthy-minded boys dribbling over Page Three girls

. . . .

While Bazzer's might begin:

> Dear Paul,
> Terry's at it again! Just because we were having a giggle over some Page Threes, she stirred up enough trouble

Read

Read out your letter to the rest of the group, in character.
Compare the letters to see how people look at facts from their own point of view.

. . . .

Drama Ideas

When you are 'in role' you are playing a part. In a **role reversal**, two people play each other's parts.
In pairs, explore some of these role reversal situations through improvisation.

1   Boy-Girl Situations

- A boy goes to a disco to dance with friends. He is approached and 'chatted up' by a very pushy girl, whom he despises.
- A boy wants to take a job and advance his career. His partner thinks that a man's place is in the home.

2   Boy-Boy Situations

- Two boys complain to each other that their partners come home drunk and beat them up.
- Two boys complain that their partners are always going off on business trips and are neglecting them.

3   Girl-Girl Situations

- Two girls are in a pub. They discuss their feeling that the exploitation of men is rubbish. What's wrong with Page Three boys?
- Two teenage girls discuss boys. 'He's got a bad reputation'; 'you have to treat them rough'; 'they love it', etc.

Make up your own role reversal situations and improvise them.

NB The boys must not put on a 'female' voice when doing these improvisations. The point of these role plays is to discover if there are any differences of role between boys and girls.

A Paper War

Character

Write

Are you surprised that DG should turn on Caf and the Tigers? Look back over the other plays (including those in **Paper Tigers**, if you can) and make a list of all the things that show that DG is not trustworthy.

Think

Why is Caf more upset than DG about the meaning of 'Paper Tigers'? Look back at the other plays to discover reasons for this.

Read

Read this 'fact file' on Ms Anne Thrope:

Fact File

Name	Anne Thrope
Age	25
Hair	Blonde
Height	1.52 m
Eyes	Blue
Weight	58.2 kg
Clothes	Business suits, always wears a skirt, not trousers. Court shoes or high heels

Write

Imagine that you have just interviewed Ms Anne Thrope for a job with Transglobal News. You have to prepare a report for your boss on the interview.
Describe her.
What did you ask?
What were her replies?
Why have you decided to recommend her for the job?

Theme: Competition

Talk

Shammy accuses Mal's gang of being greedy in trying to take over Mr Ali's shop. What do you think of Transglobal News' attempt to put Mr Ali out of business? Do you think the methods they employ are fair? What are your reasons for this?

· ·

Ambitions

Think

How does Mr Ali behave towards the Tigers in this play, and how do they
behave towards him?
Now think about Big Mal's gang and Ms Anne Thrope. How does their
behaviour towards each other compare with that of Mr Ali and the Tigers?
(Use examples from the play to back up your ideas.)

Write

From the following phrases and words, make a list of the things the people
who run Transglobal News want, in order of priority, with the most important
thing first.

Peace   Being the best at everything   Helping others   Making money

Happy marriage   Taking what you can get

Holidays

Looking after poor people   Position

Power   Success   Social equality

Good education   Getting praise   Health

Coming out on top

Kindness to animals   Protecting the environment

Discuss

Now decide in groups what *you* consider to be the most important things in
life.

Write

Make a list of these important things.
Compare the two lists you have made.
Compare your lists with those of other groups. How do they compare?
What are the implications of any differences?

Motivation

Think

In the play, Ms Thrope puts Mal and his gang through a motivation exercise.
What is the purpose of the exercise?
American football and basketball coaches also use this kind of motivation. Can
you think of any other organizations who use it?
Do you think that this motivation is harmless, or is it a form of brainwashing?

• •

Name-calling

Discuss

The Tigers feel betrayed when they learn the true meaning of their name.
Sharon tells them the results of their own name calling on her.

Have you ever been called names?
Have you ever called anyone else names?
Why do you think people call each other names?

'Sticks and stones may break my bones, but names will never hurt me.'
Discuss whether you think this old saying is true or not.

Anorexia

Research

What is anorexia nervosa? Find out as much as you can about it.
Sharon becomes anorexic because she is teased about being overweight, but in
fact most people who suffer from anorexia have never been overweight.
Anorexia is a psychological disorder: it is a disease caused not by a germ or
virus, but by a person's mind.

Other psychological disorders include:

- phobias (these are fears such as arachnophobia – fear of spiders)
- acute nervousness
- learning difficulties
- stammering
- stealing (kleptomania).

Discuss

How do we treat people who suffer from psychological disorders? Are people
who suffer from these given more sympathy than people with diseases like
cancer? If so, should they be?

• •

Drama Ideas

Role Play

The Tigers decide that they ought to interview Mal's gang before agreeing to allow them to work for Mr Ali. There will be others applying for the jobs, who are not members of either gang.

In groups, choose to be either:
a Tiger
a member of Mal's gang
a newcomer.

The Tigers: decide on the questions that you wish to ask the applicants, to make sure you choose the best candidate.

Mal's gang: talk about how you can convince the Tigers that you are the best people for the job.

Other applicants (you may wish to be DG): you have to think of reasons why you would make a better newspaper deliverer than a member of Mal's gang.

Every new applicant should have:
- a suitable nickname
- at least one skill that makes them a good candidate for the job.

Use the hot seating method to help you create these characters.
Hold the interviews.
After the interviews, the Tigers decide whom they wish to take on.

Acknowledgements

The English lyrics of 'My Way' by Paul Anka, © 1967 Ste. des Nells, & Intersong Music Ltd., London, are reproduced by permission of International Music Publications.

The illustrations are by Phillip Burrows and the handwriting is by Elitta Fell. The publishers would like to thank Ulrike Preuss/Format for permission to reproduce the photograph on p147.

· ·

Other plays in this series include:

Across the Barricades   ISBN 0 19 831272 5
Joan Lingard   adapted by David Ian Neville

The Burston School Strike   ISBN 0 19 8312741
Roy Nevitt

The Demon Headmaster   ISBN 0 19 831270 9
Gillian Cross   adapted by Adrian Flynn

Frankenstein   ISBN 0 19 831267 9
Mary Shelley   adapted by Philip Pullman

Hot Cakes   ISBN 0 19 831273 3
Adrian Flynn

Paper Tigers   ISBN 0 19 831268 7
Steve Barlow and Steve Skidmore

A Question of Courage   ISBN 0 19 831271 7
Marjorie Darke   adapted by Bill Lucas and Brian Keaney

The Teen Commandments   ISBN 0 19 831275 X
Kelvin Reynolds

The Turbulent Term of Tyke Tiler   ISBN 0 19 831269 5
adapted from her own novel by Gene Kemp